The New

Enchantment of America

SOUTH CAROLINA

By Allan Carpenter

 CHILDRENS PRESS, CHICAGO

ACKNOWLEDGMENTS

For assistance in the preparation of the revised edition, the author thanks:
CONNIE BOINEAU, Editorial Assistant, South Carolina Department of Parks, Recreation and Tourism.

American Airlines— Anne Vitaliano, Director of Public Relations; *Capitol Historical Society,* Washington, D. C.; *Newberry Library,* Chicago, Dr. Lawrence Towner, Director; *Northwestern University Library,* Evanston, Illinois; *United Airlines—* John P. Grember, Manager of Special Promotions; Joseph P. Hopkins, Manager, News Bureau; Carl Provorse, *Carpenter Publishing House.*

UNITED STATES GOVERNMENT AGENCIES: *Department of Agriculture—* Robert Hailstock, Jr., Photography Division, Office of Communication; Donald C. Schuhart, Information Division, Soil Conservation Service. *Army—* Doran Topolosky, Public Affairs Office, Chief of Engineers, Corps of Engineers. *Department of Interior—* Louis Churchville, Director of Communications; EROS Space Program— Phillis Wiepking, Community Affairs; Charles Withington, Geologist; Mrs. Ruth Herbert, Information Specialist; Bureau of Reclamation; National Park Service— Fred Bell and the individual sites; Fish and Wildlife Service— Bob Hines, Public Affairs Office. *Library of Congress—* Dr. Alan Fern, Director of the Department of Research; Sara Wallace, Director of Publications; Dr. Walter W. Ristow, Chief, Geography and Map Division; Herbert Sandborn, Exhibits Officer. *National Archives—* Dr. James B. Rhoads, Archivist of the United States; Albert Meisel, Assistant Archivist for Educational Programs; David Eggenberger, Publications Director; Bill Leary, Still Picture Reference; James Moore, Audio-Visual Archives. *United States Postal Service—* Herb Harris, Stamps Division.

For assistance in the preparation of the first edition, the author thanks:
Consultant Mrs. Arney R. Childs, South Carolina Editor, Colliers Merit Encyclopedia; Robert E. McNair, Governor; Mrs. A.D. Oliphant, Greenville; South Carolina Education Association; Caldwell Withers, Withers and Carson, Columbia; State Development Board, Columbia.

Illustrations on the preceding pages:
Cover photograph: Peach Orchard, USDA, Soil Conservation Service
Page 1: Commemorative stamps of historic interest
Pages 2-3: Middleton Gardens, South Carolina Department of Parks, Recreation and Tourism
Page 3: (Map) USDI Geological Survey
Pages 4-5: Charleston and Fort Sumter National Monument Area, EROS Space Photo, USDI Geological Survey, EROS Data Center

Project Editor, Revised Edition:
 Joan Downing
Assistant Editor, Revised Edition:
 Mary Reidy

Library of Congress Cataloging in Publication Data

Carpenter, John Allan, 1917-
 South Carolina.

 (His The new enchantment of America)
 Includes index.
 SUMMARY: An introduction to the Palmetto State, including its history, natural resources, famous citizens, and places of interest.
 1. South Carolina—Juvenile literature. [1. South Carolina]
 I. Title. II. Series.
 F269.C3 1979 975.7 79-11453
 ISBN 0-516-04140-1

Contents

A TRUE STORY TO SET THE SCENE 9
Our Leader Frank and Bold

LAY OF THE LAND 11
From ''Sahkanga'' to the Sea—Other Natural Features—Climate

FOOTSTEPS ON THE LAND 15
Indian Ancestors—Feeble Beginnings—A Town for King Charles—Growing Pains—A Royal Colony—Wars and Rumors of Wars

YESTERDAY AND TODAY 25
South Carolina and The Revolution—A New State—Prelude to Conflict—''Death Could Not Terrify, Nor Defeat Dishonor''—''Rule of the Robbers''—An End to Reconstruction—A Modern State—The People of South Carolina

NATURAL TREASURES 43
Animal—Vegetable—Mineral

PEOPLE USE THEIR TREASURES 47
Keeping Things Spinning—''And on that Farm They Raised . . .''—Lightweight Wonder and Others—Transportation and Communication

HUMAN TREASURES 55
The President—The Statesman—The General; Robin Hood of the Revolution—How Does Your Garden Grow?—Other Public Figures—Such Ingenious People—Such Creative People—Such Interesting People

TEACHING AND LEARNING 67

ENCHANTMENT OF SOUTH CAROLINA 71
''Unlike Any Others''—''Cultural Center of the New World,'' Charleston—Charleston's ''Riot of Bloom''—The Rest of the Low-country—The Capital—The Rest of the Middle Country—The Up-country

HANDY REFERENCE SECTION 88
Instant Facts—You Have a Date With History—Thinkers, Doers, Fighters—Governors of the State of South Carolina

INDEX...92

PICTURE CREDITS......................................96

ABOUT THE AUTHOR 96

Francis Marion Offers His Humble Meal,
a famous painting by John Blake White.

A True Story to Set the Scene

OUR LEADER FRANK AND BOLD

The scene painted by the artist was an unusual one. In the center was a table made of a few rough boards supported by four yoked sticks. On the table were a few blackened baked potatoes. A shortish man in rather soiled knee breeches and a dignified man in the immaculate crimson and white uniform of a British officer were both gesturing toward the table. Behind them were a few rough-looking men in a setting of a dark and mysterious forest.

This painting was supposed to be a typical scene in the unusual life of Francis Marion, America's most successful guerrilla fighter of the Revolution, who flitted about the swamps of eastern South Carolina like a shadow.

During the day, he and his men lay low at their Snow Island lair or at the Peyre Plantation. Then at night they came from their hideout, silently and ruthlessly, attacked at midnight, killed, destroyed, and sent the enemy into panicky flight. Once again they disappeared into the depths of the Pee Dee or Santee river wildernesses where no one could follow them.

For a time Marion and his men stood almost alone against the British in South Carolina, cutting the line of British supplies between Camden and Charleston, running McLeroth's forces out of Williamsburg, challenging the great British General Lord Cornwallis himself, and as American General Nathanael Greene said, generally "flushing the bird."

Francis Marion was born in Berkeley County, South Carolina, at Goatfield Plantation in St. John's Parish in 1732. He had little formal education and even less strict military instruction, but he seemed to have been born with a knowledge of military strategy. After his brilliant wartime service, he returned to his Pond Bluff Plantation and died on February 27, 1795. He was buried in the family cemetery, at Gabriel's Plantation on Belle Isle.

To the people of South Carolina, Francis Marion was a hero, the Robin Hood of the Revolution. But his death was little noted

elsewhere, and it appeared that his name might soon be forgotten in American history.

Then in 1809 Parson Mason Locke Weems published his biography of Marion, based on the "documents furnished by his brother-in-arms, Brigadier General P. Horry," as Weems stated on the title page. Parson Weems told many interesting stories concerning General Marion. One of the stories was about the British officer who was invited to visit Marion's swamp camp under a flag of truce. The general offered his visitor a potato baked in the coals of the campfire and served on a slab of bark. "But General, surely this cannot be your usual fare." "Indeed, sir, it is," said Marion, "and we are fortunate on this occasion, entertaining company, to have more than our usual fare."

Parson Weems' story goes on to say that the officer was so impressed with the sacrifices the Americans were making that he resigned his commission and went back to England.

Artist John Blake White painted the famous picture of the baked potatoes. He said he remembered Marion, and had sat on his knee as a little boy. The picture was later printed on Confederate money.

Whether or not the Weems' stories were true, his book, the picture, and other accounts quickly gained worldwide fame for Marion. He has grown into an almost legendary figure, ever more heroic and romantic with every passing year.

Marion was much more than a picturesque character, however. Known as the "Swamp Fox," he made a real contribution to the British defeat in the South.

The story of Francis Marion is one of the true stories of the enchantment of South Carolina, and most Americans will still thrill to the words of William Cullen Bryant:

> *Our band is few, but true and tried,*
> *Our leader frank and bold:*
> *The British soldier trembles*
> *When Marion's name is told.*

Lay of the Land

FROM "SAHKANGA" TO THE SEA

The Indians called South Carolina's mountains *Sahkanga,* which means the "great blue hills of God." Today these are known by the slightly less poetic name of the Blue Ridge Mountains. The Blue Ridge Province is one of the three main topographic regions of the state, occupying about 500 square miles (1,295 square kilometers). Here the rugged terrain climbs to a high point of 3,560 feet (1,085 meters) on the misty summit of Sassafras Mountain.

The middle region of the state is known as the Piedmont or Midlands. South Carolina's flat land stretching from the sea to the Piedmont is called the Coastal Plain. Dividing the Coastal Plain from the Piedmont is a line of bluffs or continuous ridges known as the Fall Line. This cuts the state into two regions of roughly equal areas, generally called up-country and low-country.

In extremely ancient times the Piedmont and Blue Ridge were part of a region known as Appalachia, which rose to great heights. Over the eons these heights were worn away by erosion, only to be lifted up again by the great primeval forces beneath the surface of the earth. The present-day Blue Ridge is what is left of one of these mountain upheavals. It is so very old that it probably has been worn down by erosion to less than half its original height.

The present Fall Line was once the seacoast, but such a vast amount of rocks, sand, and soil were washed down from the mountains and the Piedmont that the shallow sea near the shore began to fill up, forming the Coastal Plain. However, the Coastal Plain rose and fell several times until the sea covered it again and again, leaving additional layers of sand, soil, and rocks.

Comparatively few fossils have left their record of the plant and animal life of ancient times in South Carolina. There are almost no fossils found above the Fall Line. Mammoths, sharks' teeth, elephant skeletons, and other remains have been found in the Coastal Plains.

South Carolina, with a total of 31,055 square miles (80,432 square kilometers), today is one of four states in the nation bordered by only two other states. The border with North Carolina is very irregular—probably the most irregular state boundary that is not based mainly on a natural feature such as a river. The small section of the Catawba River is the only river boundary between the two states. On the other hand, the boundary with Georgia is all river, beginning with the Chattooga River on the north and west and continuing with the Tugaloo and Savannah rivers on the southwest.

OTHER NATURAL FEATURES

Rushing bright blue over mountain rocks, running yellow with clay in the up-country, and flowing like black glass beneath the cypresses of the low-country, the rivers come to the sea. In addition to the Savannah, the other main river systems of the state are the Santee, Edisto, and the Pee Dee. The main tributaries of the Santee are the Wateree and the Congaree. The principal branches of the Pee Dee are the Little Pee Dee and the Lynches. Other rivers include the Black, Waccamaw, Cooper, Ashley, Combahee, Coosawhatchie, Broad, and Saluda.

Stretching out into the sea are more than one hundred fifty low sandy barrier islands such as Bull Island, Isle of Palms, Sullivans Island, Edisto, Hunting, Fripp, and Hilton Head. The regular coastline of South Carolina is 187 miles (301 kilometers) long. The shoreline stretches for 2,876 miles (4,628 kilometers).

The principal inland bodies of water of South Carolina are the large man-made lakes or reservoirs—Greenwood, Catawba, Wateree, Santee-Cooper, Murray, Clark Hill, and Hartwell. The last two are shared with Georgia. To these must be added interconnected Lake Marion and Lake Moultrie, both naturally formed, but increased in size and volume by the Santee-Cooper Dam.

In addition there are, of course, smaller lakes and thousands of farm ponds in the state, all these together making a total water area of over 783 square miles (2,028 square kilometers) for South Carolina.

Mountains and lakes are typical of the state's geography.

CLIMATE

Though the temperature sometimes dips to sub-zero in the mountains or climbs to a sweltering 100 degrees Fahrenheit (37.8 degrees Celsius) or more along the coast, the climate is generally mild throughout the state, with the coastal climate usually described as "sub-tropical." The state's growing season ranges from nine months on the coast to seven months in the mountains. Rain fall is abundant and well distributed, lightest along the coast and heaviest in the mountains, averaging 47.7 inches (about 120 centimeters) per year for the state. However, the average shows that only about 95 of the 365 days are rainy. No very large regions have ever been flooded by excessive rains.

Young women in antebellum costumes in the garden of Darby Plantation.
Plantation tours can be made throughout the state in March and April.

Footsteps on the Land

INDIAN ANCESTORS

The horse had always been the *sachem's* (chief's) favorite, and now he must follow his master to the land of the Great Spirit so that the old sachem would have a horse there. A terrified neigh and it was all over. The sorrowing Indians bound their leader's body to his faithful beast and began to throw handfuls of sand over horse and master. Soon only a mound of sand was visible. No one knows how many others were buried in the same place in the same way, but today Indian Hill is called a "mountain" by the local settlers.

This mound is one of the comparatively few remaining reminders of the peoples who once possessed South Carolina. Not very much is known about those who were there before the Europeans came. A group known as Archaic-Early Woodland people left such evidences of themselves as the Seewee Indian Shell Mound on Bull Bay. The mound is made up of discarded shells of oyster, conch, clam, and even freshwater mussels. There are also fragments of clay pottery.

In historical times there are records of more than twenty-eight well-defined groups who occupied South Carolina. These were members of five separate great language groups.

The most numerous and powerful of all were the Cherokee, who occupied an enormous tract in the highlands extending over much of South Carolina and the other Appalachian states. Probably next in importance were the confederated groups headed by the Catawba nation. These were related to the Sioux nation of the Western plains; they included the Peedee, Congaree, Wateree, Seewee, Santee, Winyah, Sampit, Cheraw, Waxhaw, and Esaw.

Coastal groups were known as the Cusabo Confederacy. The individual Cusabo were Combahee, Edisto, Ashepoo, Wimbee, St. Helena, Bohicket, Wando, Stono, Kiawah, Etiwan, and the wandering Yamasee. They were not very powerful. Sometimes included in this group were the Coosa, who lived somewhat farther inland.

A group of newcomers to the middle Savannah River region were the fierce Westo, much feared by their neighbors due to their

15

reputation as cannibals. The upper Savannah region was the hunting ground of the Hogologee, a division of the Yuchi.

After European settlement, some Indians moved in from Spanish regions farther to the south. These included the Apalachee and the Yamasee. Other latecomers were the Nunda Wadigi, an Iroquois group that came from New York in 1630.

The Cherokee, also Iroquois-related, were the most highly developed and cultured Indians of the group and among the most advanced of all the Indians in what is now the United States. However, most of the Indians had advanced far beyond the ways of the Stone Age in at least some of their activities.

Most of them lived in fortified communities, protected by strong palisades, made generally of vertical poles. Within these walls the houses were made of frame covered with bark in the lowlands and sometimes of logs among the more advanced groups, particularly the Cherokee. The largest building was the council house, used also for worship and community activities. Here burned the constant fire that was renewed once each year with much ceremony.

Many food crops were grown and cultivated, textiles and feathers were woven, and skins were dressed for garments. Most groups had skilled basket makers, and pottery was nicely made but without a glaze. Canoes were of the dugout type.

The councils consisted mostly of the old men, who did most of the governing. The position of the sachems varied; some had little authority, while others were almost dictators.

Two of the most interesting stories of the South Carolina Indians have to do with epic journeys.

The proud and independent Seewee had many grievances against the Europeans. They had heard much of the great king who ruled so far away, and decided that they must go to him directly and appeal for justice. They constructed huge canoes, and the whole group set out on a journey to the east, none of them knew exactly where. They paddled into the sunrise. A captured pirate told of his amazement at seeing a flotilla of Indian canoes far out at sea. Nothing more was ever heard of the Seewee. This poignant and stirring tale of courage and determination is probably unique in history.

Entirely different was the voyage of seven Cherokee chiefs who actually did go to London in the 1730s. The people of London treated them royally; they were entertained at many lavish affairs. The king received them with all possible ceremony. When they returned to their villages from the palaces of England, they never tired of recounting the many wonders they had seen.

FEEBLE BEGINNINGS

South Carolina can boast of a unique distinction in history, although a fleeting one. Captain Lucas Vásquez de Ayllón sprang ashore in 1526 at what is now Winyah Bay, thrust into the sand the flagpole bearing the flag of Spain and claimed the land in the name of his king. He had brought with him from Santo Domingo a well-rounded group of five hundred colonists, including doctors, priests, and slaves, along with cattle, sheep, and other animals. They called their settlement San Miguel de Guadalupe. However, within a few months two thirds of the people, including Ayllón, had died of disease, Indian attack, and slave revolt, and the pitiful remainder sailed away. This short-lived community is considered the first European settlement on the coast of North America.

In 1540-41 Hernando de Soto's destructive expedition made its way into what is now western South Carolina. Near present-day Silver Bluff they were received and kindly treated by Indian Princess Cofitachiqui, who fed the starving forces and presented de Soto with a beautiful string of pearls. He repaid her kindness by carrying her away as a captive, and his army left a trail of disease and misfortune in its wake.

The first Protestant settlement in America was made by Huguenots at Parris Island in 1652 under the direction of French naval officer Jean Ribaut. After they had made a log and earth fort, Ribaut sailed back to France for reinforcements, leaving twenty-six men to hold the fort. When it appeared that Ribaut was not coming back, the men mutinied, built a crude ship, using their shirts for sails, and started away. When their food was gone, they decided to

Delegation of Cherokee Chiefs, 1730.

kill and eat one of their own number. They chose the victim by lot, and it turned out to be the man who had made the suggestion. Later they were picked up by a British ship and returned to France.

In order to maintain their claim of ownership of all the Americas, the Spanish planted about twenty forts (sometimes called mission-forts) up the coast from Florida, including St. George's Bay close to present-day Charleston, but wars with the Indians and other European powers kept these from succeeding.

A TOWN FOR KING CHARLES

England claimed much the same territory, and Charles I of England granted "all America from sea to sea between the 36 and 31 parallels of Latitude under the name of Carolana" to Sir Robert Heath. However, not much more was done until Charles II, in gratitude for the help of his friends in gaining the crown, offered a charter for this same region to eight of his most loyal friends, who were known as the lords proprietors. In honor of their patron they named the region Carolina. The grant included both of the present-day Carolinas as well as much of other present states farther west.

As soon as possible, the eight noble lords sent explorers into their territory. One of these was Dr. Henry Woodward, who stayed in the region and became one of the greatest authorities on the Indians and the resources of the country. He has been called the "first permanent European settler in the Carolinas."

In 1670 Dr. Woodward met 148 people sent by the proprietors and gave them great assistance in making a settlement at Albermarle Point, which they called Charles Towne to honor the king. This was the first permanent European settlement in South Carolina. On the death of Colonel William Sayle, who had been appointed governor, Captain Joseph West took command of the new colony.

The proprietors originally planned to govern the colony somewhat on the English feudal model. They called on philosopher John Locke to write their *Fundamental Constitutions*. These laws provided for three classes of nobility—landgraves, caciques, and barons—to have huge estates in the new country. The Episcopal church was to have state support, but other faiths would be tolerated. However, the feudal system never was really accepted by the colonists.

After ten years, the community of Charles Towne was moved to its present location, where it eventually was renamed Charleston; there it grew rapidly. For many years Charles Towne was the center of trade and colonization of the whole area. Within twenty years its trade with the Indians had extended even as far as the Mississippi River.

GROWING PAINS

Rice was introduced from Madagascar in 1685 and became a bumper crop. Indigo was another prized commodity for export to Europe. The first slaves were brought in 1670, and their numbers grew as the plantations flourished and required more workers.

This was a period when many things, including the Indians, foreign nations, and pirates, threatened the lives and welfare of the colony. In 1686 Spanish forces from Florida attacked the colony. A force of five hundred men was raised to retaliate on the Spanish capital of St. Augustine, but the lords proprietors would not permit this because they had a thriving trade with Spain.

In 1702 Spain and France joined in a war against England, and in 1706 the two nations sent a five-warship fleet to capture Charles Towne, calling on Governor Nathaniel Johnson to surrender within an hour. "I do not need a minute to decide. I hold this province for Her Majesty, Queen Anne of England. I am ready to die in its defense but not to surrender it," the governor replied.

Whether true or not, an interesting story is told that the governor then conducted the envoy who brought the surrender demands on a tour of the city's defenses. As they moved about he blindfolded the envoy, then uncovered his eyes to show him every strong point. The same group of troops was hurried from one place to another so that at each point the envoy saw a large garrison. He hurried back to his fleet to report that Charles Towne had a very strong defense force. Fooled by this trick, after some fighting, the enemy fleet sailed away.

The Indians had watched with growing distrust as the colonists spread over more and more of their land. In 1715, fifteen thousand Indians took to the warpath in a struggle known as the Yamasee War. They massacred ninety settlers of Pocotaligo and then a hundred at Port Royal. The whole garrison was wiped out at St. Stephens, and other locations were hard hit.

Governor Charles Craven was able to stop an attack at the Stono River. Then another settlers' group was able to sail up to the principal Indian village near Pocotaligo and destroy it. Meanwhile another force of Indians was coming down from the north. These were defeated in a sharp battle with the European forces led by Captain George Chicken. After about a year of fighting, the Yamasee War came to an end. However, four hundred settlers had died, and Charles Towne was about the only settlement left of any consequence.

Charleston before 1739, a watercolor by Bishop Roberts.

Not as dangerous, but almost as troublesome, were the pirates who swarmed along the coast in unbelievable numbers. Local officials in many places protected the pirates and shared in their booty. No ships were safe from pirates, who captured their cargoes and killed passengers and crew or held them for ransom. Famous pirates such as Blackbeard, Richard Worley, and Stede Bonnet made life miserable for honest men.

At last an expedition from Charles Towne led by William Rhett and Robert Johnson made its way up the coast and defeated the pirates in two severe battles. After a stupendous fight, Blackbeard was

21

killed. Worley also died and Bonnet was captured. The captives were tried and sentenced to death.

The nation has probably never seen another such grisly procession as that formed by the twenty-two pirates who were hanged near the Battery in Charles Towne in one day, led by the notorious Stede Bonnet, who was first to die. The noose had scarcely stopped swinging from one execution before another neck was inserted for the last ghastly moments. Altogether forty-nine pirates were executed in a single month; a total of sixty died.

A ROYAL COLONY

The proprietors had become inefficient and greedy. They refused to aid the colonists in the Indian wars, refused to pay for any of the costs of the recent wars, neglected the colonists in many other ways, raised their rents 400 percent, and even demanded the lands that the colonists took away from the Yamasee during the war.

In an angry mood the colonists revolted against the proprietors' agents in 1719 and elected a governor of their own—James Moore. They hurried a representative to the king to explain their actions and ask to be made a royal colony. During this period the colony was virtually self-governing.

The king was sympathetic to those who had revolted, and South Carolina was made a royal colony with Robert Johnson as first governor.

The years that followed were ones of truly remarkable progress. Immigration was encouraged with grants of land, and large numbers of German, Swiss, Scotch-Irish, and other groups came, mostly into the mid-country up to the Fall Line.

As settlement pushed farther inland, the Cherokee became concerned. Just when it appeared there might be much trouble with the Cherokee, an extraordinary man arrived in the back country. This was Sir Alexander Cuming, who alone persuaded the Cherokee to sign a key treaty of peace.

When he told the settlers of his plan, they thought he was crazy, but Cuming went to the Indian village of Keowee, burst into the council chamber where outsiders were forbidden and made a rousing speech, ending with the invitation to drink the health of their "Great White Chief," the king of England. The leaders were greatly impressed and agreed to meet with other Indian leaders.

Cuming went to many other Indian villages, repeating his performance and requesting them to come to the treaty meeting at Keowee. The meeting was a great success, with much feasting and the vowing of loyalty to the great king and peace with his colonists. Cuming became known to the Cherokee as "The Great Warrior." It was at his urging that the Indians sent their representatives to England to meet the king.

For almost thirty years after this extraordinary feat of personal diplomacy, the Cherokee kept their pledge of peace with the South Carolina colonists.

The colony continued to progress in spite of such disasters as the "Great Mortality" of 1749 in which hundreds died of a disease now thought to have been influenza, "ye dred smallpox," and other diseases which took a great toll.

Landholders prospered, and many lived lives of great luxury on sumptuous plantations, where fantastic gardens were laid out by the best landscape architects, and the homes were built and planned for the most elegant of tastes. Charles Towne became the cultural center of the colonies, even surpassing Boston and Philadelphia in almost every field except literature and science. Most of these accomplishments were based on the income from an export trade which by 1768 totaled a fifth of all the exports of the thirteen colonies.

WARS AND RUMORS OF WARS

During the French and Indian War, French agents did their best to convince the Cherokee that some day they would be attacked by the English from such locations as Fort Prince George, near present-day Pickens. The Cherokee had contributed the land on which that fort had been built. Leaders of the Cherokee, such as Chief

Attakullakulla, tried to persuade their people that the French were leading them astray, but at last the Cherokee disregarded all warnings and went on the warpath. Fort Prince George fell, and settlers were attacked in many brutal raids such as the Long Cane Massacre, when one-hundred-fifty settlers were attacked and many killed or captured.

Later, Fort Prince George was retaken, and the British forces began a ruthless campaign to destroy Cherokee settlements and crops. The Cherokee were forced to surrender, and in 1761 Chief Attakullakulla headed a delegation of Cherokee chiefs who went to Charles Towne to surrender. Much of the strength of the Cherokee had been broken permanently.

In the growing dispute with the mother country, prosperous South Carolina had fewer causes for complaint than some of the colonists to the north. However, the people of South Carolina had become increasingly independent, and their Commons House of Representatives considered itself as independent as the British House of Commons.

When the British began to tax the colonies without their consent, South Carolina joined the other colonies in protesting. South Carolina sent delegates to the Stamp Act Congress in New York in 1765. A group of colonists occupied Fort Johnson in 1765 and threatened to sink a ship bringing in the tax stamps. The captain sailed away in face of this threat. The flag used by the colonists in this scuffle was said to be the first independent flag ever used in any of the colonies. Charles Towne had its own "tea party" in 1774, when a shipload of the only item on which the tax remained was thrown into the sea. However, many shiploads of tea were confiscated and stored. Sale of the stored tea three years later helped to finance the Revolution.

In 1774 a convention met at Charles Towne and elected five delegates to the First Continental Congress. South Carolina delegates were also sent to the Second Congress in 1775. A provincial congress took over South Carolina's government in 1775, and the royal governor fled. South Carolina prepared for the war that must swiftly come.

Yesterday and Today

SOUTH CAROLINA AND THE REVOLUTION

Some of the most severe fighting and much of the worst suffering of the Revolutionary War took place in South Carolina. Altogether, 137 battles were fought there. One hundred three of these were fought by South Carolina men alone, without help from the other colonies.

The fighting began on an exciting and victorious note. A small fort of palmetto trunks had been only partly completed on Sullivans Island at the entrance to Charles Towne harbor when on June 28, 1776, a fleet of eleven British warships attacked. Colonel William Moultrie led the colonists in a brilliant defense.

Almost at once American fire put the *Bristol* out of commission and killed 100 of her men. On that ship the fleeing royal governor of South Carolina, Sir William Campbell, was killed, and the fleet commander, Sir Peter Parker, had his pants burned off and was wounded twice. Three British ships went aground. A British landing force of 3,000 men under Sir Henry Clinton and Lord Charles Cornwallis was held off by 780 Americans. The British withdrew with 200 killed, compared to the 12 American dead. South Carolina was safe from another major British attack for almost four years.

Over the fort had flown the South Carolina flag—three white crescents on a blue background. Because the palmettos of the fort had absorbed the British cannonballs like a sponge, a white palmetto was added to the flag. The local hero of this battle was Sergeant William Jasper, who replaced the fort's flag at the peril of his life. In honor of the commander, the fort was named Moultrie.

Six days after the battle, the Declaration of Independence was signed. South Carolina's signers were Thomas Lynch, Jr., Thomas Heyward, Jr., Arthur Middleton, and Edward Rutledge.

During the period from 1776 to 1780 most of the war action in South Carolina was carried on with the Cherokee Indians who had allied themselves with the British or with those who had remained loyal to the king—Tories.

A British drummer, part of a re-inactment of the Revolution.

Then in March, 1780, the British laid siege to Charles Towne, which still had not taken the present spelling of its name. In May, the city, under its commander General Benjamin Lincoln, was forced to surrender. Most of the American troops in the Carolinas were taken captive. American General Horatio Gates hurriedly formed an army to try to recapture the lost territory, but he was defeated and the British were in control of South Carolina. After Colonel Abraham Buford's troops surrendered, the British under Colonel Banastre Tarleton massacred them near Lancaster. Through this act Tarleton earned the nickname "Bloody Tarleton," and the cry "Remember Tarleton" helped to rally Americans throughout the rest of the war.

During these difficult times, American hopes were kept alive by guerrilla forces. The guerrillas had so little in the way of supplies that their wives had to melt down their pewter and mold it into bullets.

The most brilliant guerrilla leader in American history was General Francis Marion. He had learned his fighting methods in the Cherokee wars. He earned his nickname the Swamp Fox because he could slip through the damp lowlands and make his kill as cunningly

Banastre Tarleton, or "Bloody Tarleton," painted by Sir Jashua Reynolds.

as a fox. Colonel Tarleton once said that the Devil himself could not catch the Swamp Fox. Marion and his men would come out of the thickets to strike at a British column or supply train and then after doing as much damage as possible would disappear again into the dense junglelike forests.

Among Marion's more unusual victories was that at Fort Watson. Marion wanted to attack the fort but had no cannon, so during a single night he and his men built a tall log tower overlooking the fort. In the morning they were in position to pour a deadly hail of small-arms fire on the enemy until they surrendered.

The guerrilla leader in the middle country was Thomas Sumter, known as "the Gamecock," and in the upper country the leader was Andrew Pickens. Their constant attacks did much to bring about the later fall of the British.

The Scotch-Irish settlers of the Piedmont region had been occupied with Indian troubles. They had not taken much interest in the larger war on the coast. However, General Lord Cornwallis sent Major Patrick Ferguson to the Piedmont, and he sent word to the mountain men under Colonels Isaac Shelby, John Sevier, William Campbell, and Benjamin Cleveland that "if they did not desist from their opposition to the British arms, and take protection under his standard, he would march his army over the mountains, hang their leaders, and lay their country waste with fire and sword."

The frontiersmen assembled quickly in hunting clothes, with knapsacks, blankets, and long hunting rifles, most of them mounted but some on foot. They took off on a twelve-day march to meet Ferguson, gathering new forces as they went. A picked force of nine hundred men caught up with Ferguson on the slopes of Kings Mountain north of York. Ferguson fortified a ridge of the mountain and declared that "God Almighty could not drive him from it."

Ferguson, known as the best shot in the British army, had invented the first breech-loading rifle, and many of his troops were equipped with this fearsome new weapon.

Less well-equipped, the Americans surrounded the ridge; Colonel Campbell shouted "Shoot like hell and fight like devils," and the Battle of Kings Mountain began. During the bloody one-hour fight the mountaineers gained a complete and stunning victory. Ferguson was killed, and his entire force was killed, wounded, or captured. American losses were only twenty-eight killed.

This victory was one of the turning points of the war. It upset the British timetable and threw Lord Cornwallis on the defensive. During one of the darkest periods of the Revolution, it brought an immediate rise in patriotic spirit, upset the Southern Tories, and renewed American resistance in the Carolinas.

General Nathanael Greene arrived to take command of American forces in the South and sent General Daniel Morgan to capture British outposts. Cornwallis sent the hated Colonel Tarleton to meet Morgan. On January 17, 1781, they met near present-day Gaffney at a corral for cattle. American victory at the Battle of the Cowpens was another important link in the final defeat of Cornwallis.

Battle of Cowpens, *a painting in the State House.*

General Andrew Pickens organized a force of about five hundred and in a campaign of only about six weeks was able to bring the warring Cherokee under control.

Other smaller battles were fought in various parts of South Carolina until the British power had been removed, and finally, in December, 1782, the British forces were withdrawn from Charles Towne. About a year later the city changed its name to Charleston.

After tremendous hardship and the loss of most of their wealth, after a period of three years in which they had almost no state government, the people of South Carolina could look forward to peace once more.

A NEW STATE

When the Constitutional Convention met at Philadelphia, South Carolina was represented by Charles Pinckney, Pierce Butler, John Rutledge, and Charles Cotesworth Pinckney. On May 23, 1788, South Carolina adopted the federal Constitution and became the eighth state of the new United States.

In 1790 Charleston ceased to be the state capital, when the

government was moved to the new, planned city of Columbia, although some government offices did not move to Columbia until as late as 1865.

When new troubles began with Britain, South Carolina leaders, especially John C. Calhoun, were among the "War Hawks" who finally influenced the United States to enter the War of 1812. After the first American victory, the story is told that Calhoun danced a reel. One of the interesting sidelights of the war was the breathtaking ride of Colonel Wade Hampton of South Carolina. He had been chosen by General Andrew Jackson to take to Washington the news of the victory at New Orleans. Colonel had gone over 1,200 miles (1,931 kilometers) in ten days to deliver his welcome message.

Many in South Carolina had been opposed to the federal government from the beginning. When tariffs were made ever higher, and the state's business suffered, opposition grew stronger. By 1827 numbers of the state's people were talking of seceding from the Union.

Dr. Thomas Cooper of the state university is often said to have originated a plan called nullification, which was supported by Calhoun. By this plan, if a state did not agree with a federal law, it would not accept it, "nullifying" or disregarding it in the state.

To keep South Carolina from carrying out its nullification threats, President Andrew Jackson (claimed as a native of South Carolina) sent warships to Charleston. Just when it appeared that warfare might break out, Congress voted a compromise to lower the tariff rates gradually.

When war came with Mexico in 1846, South Carolina sent its famous Palmetto Regiment into the fighting. Out of eleven hundred men who volunteered for service in the war, only three hundred ever returned.

PRELUDE TO CONFLICT

The patriotism of the war years did not last long, however. The Abolitionists of the North grew increasingly determined that slavery should be done away with. Leaders of South Carolina insisted that their entire economic system was based on slavery, and they felt compelled to argue for slavery and to extend it wherever possible.

Many in the state had few or no slaves, and they had no cause to promote slavery. Others were able to see that the slave system really had outlived any economic usefulness it might have had. There were even some Abolitionists, such as Sarah and Angelina Grimkez of Charleston. Greenville was a leading center of those who supported the Northern view, encouraged by Benjamin F. Perry.

However, the overwhelming majority supported the general Southern position. At last, of course, the leaders of the state and the majority of the people agreed that there was no other course but for them to withdraw, or secede, from the United States. Governor William H. Gist sent his cousin States Rights (his baptismal name) Gist to call on Southern governors to promote their interest in secession.

A convention met at the First Baptist Church of Columbia on December 17, 1860. Because of smallpox in Columbia, it moved to Charleston. Under the chairmanship of D. F. Jamison it discussed secession for a total of three days. On the 20th, the Ordinance of Secession was approved at Charleston without an opposing vote, and South Carolina became the first state to secede. An interesting sidelight is the speech of the delegate from Edisto Island, who declared that Edisto would secede from the Union whether the rest of the state did or not. By February, 1861, enough states had followed South Carolina's secession lead to form the Confederate States of America.

"DEATH COULD NOT TERRIFY, NOR DEFEAT DISHONOR"

South Carolina began at once to prepare for war. Committees of vigilance and safety were organized; the militia was reorganized, and minutemen were prepared to maintain order. Eleven regiments of volunteers were formed during the first months of 1861.

Representatives of South Carolina in Washington had asked for

31

possession of the three Union forts in Charleston harbor—Sumter, Moultrie, and Castle Pinckney. Federal troops occupied only one of them, Fort Moultrie. Before the Union government made a reply, the Union troops were moved to Fort Sumter, a much stronger position.

Governor Francis Pickens immediately took control of Castle Pinckney, Fort Moultrie, and the Federal Arsenal at Charleston. The Union government sent the ship *Star of the West* with supplies and reinforcements for Sumter. A group of cadets from the Citadel, the Charleston military school, were holding Morris Island. As the *Star of the West* sailed by, the cadets opened fire on her. Cadet George E. Haynesworth, of the town of Sumter, is considered to have fired the very first shot of the great war that was soon to engulf the whole country. The *Star of the West* turned back before it reached Fort Sumter.

On April 12, 1861, the chimes of St. Michael's had just rung out when a shell lit up the sky and exploded over Fort Sumter. General P.G.T. Beauregard, commander of Charleston's defense, had ordered the fort to be attacked. The ring of guns and mortars around the harbor opened fire. All business in Charleston stopped. Every church steeple, housetop, and wharf in the city was crowded with people who watched tensely as the bombardment went on for thirty-four hours, until the white flag of surrender appeared and the Union garrison marched out of Fort Sumter.

After this, it was clear that war could not be avoided, and both sides stepped up their preparations.

The defense of Charleston was the most spectacular part of the war in South Carolina. Union forces besieged Charleston harbor for 567 days. "It was, and still remains, the longest siege in modern history," according to one authority. Fort Sumter under Confederate forces held out against the most modern weapons, including Requa machine guns of 24 barrels. These are supposed to have been the first rapid-fire guns ever used in warfare.

The first extensive use of submarine warfare was introduced by the Confederate defenders of Charleston, and among its successes was the Union ship *Patapsco,* torpedoed in Charleston harbor.

A diorama showing the bombardment of Fort Sumter.

Other coastal defenses fell, however. In November, 1861, Union vessels took control of Port Royal. They next tried to seize the railroad from Charleston to Savannah, Georgia, but were driven away.

However, by April, 1863, Union forces were able to blockade the entire South Carolina coast. Some of the most exciting stories of the war are concerned with the Confederate success in running supplies through this blockade, and Charleston was a main center for blockade-running.

By 1864, in addition to Port Royal, Beaufort and Morris and Folly islands, the latter two part of the defense of Charleston, had fallen to Union forces. December found General William T. Sherman moving relentlessly through South Carolina from Savannah. Everything in a 40-mile (64-kilometer) path was destroyed—homes burned, crops captured or destroyed, possessions looted. Sherman arrived at Columbia with forty thousand men on February 16, 1865, and began at once to bombard the city.

Mayor Goodwyn met the Union general at Broad Road and surrendered the capital city. Although Sherman is said to have promised to save the city, by the next night the city was burning; 84 blocks, including 1,386 buildings, fell before the flames. Sherman denied that Union troops set the fires and claimed the retiring commander of Columbia, General Wade Hampton, was responsible for them.

Charleston was evacuated on the same day, but it escaped the capital's fate of fire.

On April 9, 1865, one of the last battles in South Carolina took place at Dingles Mill, when 159 Confederates were able to stop 2,700 Union troops. On that same day, General Lee surrendered in Virginia, and the war ended.

One of the problems of the war concerned the deserters. Many of those who did not own slaves or land felt no loyalty to the state officers and others who were trying to save the slave system. Many deserted from the army almost as soon as they were drafted. This was especially true in the hill country. Often they organized into groups of renegades, and lived by plundering the local people. This was a particular problem in the Greenville area.

More than 63,000 soldiers from South Carolina served in the war with loyalty to their cause, and 25 percent died. The sacrifice of manpower is illustrated by the fact that at one time during the war there were only 500 men left in all of Columbia.

William Henry Trescot paid tribute to the state's war dead with this epitaph:

> Let the stranger
> Who may in future times
> Read this inscription
> Recognize that these were men
> Whom power could not corrupt,
> Whom death could not terrify,
> Whom defeat could not dishonor . . .
> Let the South Carolinians
> Of another generation
> Remember . . .

The priceless treasure of their memories,
Teaching all who may claim
The same birthright
That truth, courage and patriotism
Endure forever.

"RULE OF THE ROBBERS"

After the war, those who were left faced a grim future; the wealth of the state had been destroyed; the plantation system was useless. Almost every feature of life had been upset or overthrown.

At the end of the war, Governor A.G. Magrath was taken to prison, and a provisional governor appointed—Benjamin F. Perry of Greenville, who was respected by both North and South. A new constitution was written; James L. Orr of Anderson was elected governor, and the legislature approved the Thirteenth Amendment to the United States Constitution, which prohibited slavery. However, the legislature would not approve the Fourteenth Amendment.

With this refusal, the state was placed under military authority of the federal government. Everyone who had been in the armed services or held a Confederate post was denied the vote.

Those who remained free to vote then elected a new constitutional convention that approved the Fourteenth Amendment. When a new legislature was elected, military rule was removed and South Carolina again became a state.

However, according to *South Carolina, A Guide to the Palmetto State,* "Thus began the darkest period in the State's history . . . The period from 1868 to 1874 is known as the 'Rule of the Robbers,' from the fact that within these years the public debt leaped from $5,407,306 to $20,333,901. . . . Votes in the legislature were bought at prices varying from the cost of a man's liquor and cigars to that of a house and lot. Furniture, jewelry, clothing, and groceries were purchased with public funds, while patients in the state hospital actually suffered for food, and threats were made to turn convicts out of the penitentiary because they could not be fed."

Corruption
of the
Carpetbaggers,
*a cartoon
of 1877.*

Many of those who took advantage of the disorganized conditions were people from the North, known as Carpetbaggers because they had hurried south with all their possessions in a carpetbag. Others, local people who preyed on the unfortunates of both races, were known as Scalawags.

Because of the hardships and the unscrupulous people who exploited the situation to their own advantage, tension between the races increased. There were race riots in Ellenton and Laurens. The latter attracted much notoriety in the North. It was led by a Scalawag with the cry, "Matches are cheap!" Near the scene of the Laurens rioting stood the little tailor shop once used by Andrew Johnson, Reconstruction president, whose term had recently ended.

AN END TO RECONSTRUCTION

In 1876, the Democrats nominated General Wade Hampton III

36

for governor. This Confederate hero organized a group of supporters known as the Red Shirts. The general carried on a colorful campaign. At Sumter he came to the speaker's platform accompanied by a draped figure bound in chains. Suddenly the chains were thrown off to show a young woman dressed in white, representing South Carolina freed once more. The people jumped up, shouting, "Hampton or hell!"

Hampton inspired extreme loyalty in his Red Shirt followers, who went to great lengths to win his election by a scant one thousand votes over his opponent, Daniel H. Chamberlain, then the governor. Chamberlain contested the election and refused to leave the capitol. For a time South Carolina had two governors and two legislatures.

Both Chamberlain and Hampton went to Washington to press their claims with President Hayes. The story is told that Hayes suggested to Hampton that the election be held again. Hampton is said to have agreed to this if Hayes would also run in a new election. This reminded Hayes how close his own election had been, and he decided that the federal government would recognize Hampton.

When word of this reached Columbia, the celebration was reported by northern newspapermen to be one of the most enthusiastic in the history of the country. The period known as Reconstruction had finally come to an end in South Carolina. The state was the last of all the Confederate states to regain its state government free from outside interference.

A MODERN STATE

Much of the progress in the period following Reconstruction occurred in fields of invention, education, transportation, industry, and communication.

In 1881 a centennial celebration of the Battle of the Cowpens was held at Spartanburg. The claim that wartime memories were beginning to fade is verified by the fact that all of the states that were the original thirteen colonies (including the northern states) were represented in the celebration.

One of the greatest disasters in Charleston's history occurred when an earthquake rocked the city in 1886. Damage reached six million dollars, and some of the city's old buildings still carry the metal support braces used to strengthen them after the quake.

Also in 1886 a move began to strengthen the small farmers of the state and improve farm conditions. This movement was under the leadership of Benjamin R. (Pitchfork) Tillman of Edgefield. Tillman became governor in 1890 and United States senator in 1894. His rise to power brought an end to the dominating position of the old low country aristocracy, which had held power almost since the colony was first established with a feudal government.

The present constitution of South Carolina was adopted in 1895. This deprived most blacks in the state of the right to vote.

In 1901 and 1902 an important event was held in Charleston—the Interstate and West Indian Exposition. Thirty-one states took part in the exposition, and President Theodore Roosevelt visited it in 1901.

The city of Sumter made history in the field of local government in 1912 when it became the first community in the United States to be governed by the type of city organization known as the Commission-City Manager Plan.

In 1917, in the beginning of World War I, the first of the 62,000 South Carolinians who served in that war were drafted. Of these, 2,085 died. One of the most important military installations of the war was Camp Wadsworth at Spartanburg. Among many others, the famous Rainbow Division of the war was trained at Wadsworth.

A strange episode of the war was the experience of Corporal Jesse B. Gillespie of Pickens. During the drive for Cantigny in France, Corporal Gillespie was wounded severely and left for dead. He was found by the French and nursed back to life in a French hospital. Meanwhile, the United States Army had issued a death certificate stating that he had "died with honor in the service of his country May 18, 1918." This certificate still hangs in the Pickens County Courthouse. In order to become "alive" again and regain his rights as a citizen, Corporal Gillespie had to sign an affidavit that he was not dead.

The 1920 cotton crop was one of the best on record, but by 1921 the insidious boll weevil had bored its way through a third of the crop. However, although it brought disaster, the boll weevil made it necessary for farmers to produce other crops and in the end probably strengthened the state's agriculture.

Because of the kinds of industry and agriculture in the state, South Carolina did not suffer as much from the Great Depression of the thirties as some other states, although times were desperately hard. One of the major government improvements of the period was the Dreher Shoals Dam completed on the Saluda River in 1931.

During World War II 173,642 from South Carolina were in uniform. One of the first American pilots killed in action in the war was Ervin David Shaw, native of Sumter. Shaw Air Force Base at Sumter is named in his honor.

In recent years, probably the most dramatic events in the state have been concerned with the almost explosive development of the state's business. A State Development Board was created in 1945 to promote manufacturing, tourism, and other interests of the state. During the twenty years from 1940 to 1960 the port of Charleston jumped from 57th place to 14th place among all the country's ports. Much of the growth continued, at a somewhat slower pace during the decades of 1960 and 1970. In 1975, Dr. James B. Edwards took office as governor, the first Republican in that post since Reconstruction days. However, the Democratic Party regained the governor's chair in 1979.

THE PEOPLE OF SOUTH CAROLINA

South Carolina has long been noted for a "polished social life not surpassed in America." Manners and culture of the low-country aristocrats were cultivated from earliest childhood, through careful education in the best colleges of Europe, and with every advantage that wealth could afford. The Charleston accent is famous in all parts of the South.

In the up-country, the early life was typical of the frontier as it moved slowly westward. Many states had differences of opinion between the early settled regions and the back country. However, in South Carolina these differences were probably more pronounced and long-lasting than elsewhere. Today such differences are rapidly vanishing. Old traditions of witchcraft, dueling, and even segregation have vanished or are vanishing.

Today's South Carolinians are 99.6 percent native-born—probably the largest percentage of any of the states. Of the more than 28 groups of Indians, only the friendly Catawba remain in any numbers; most of them live on their reservation near Rock Hill. The 1970 census listed 2,241 Indians in South Carolina.

St. Helena Island is the center of an unusual black culture. The blacks of the area are of almost pure African stock. Many speak a dialect known as Gullah. Among their many unusual accomplishments has been the development of a number of prominent songs and spirituals. Dr. Reed Smith asserted that "Unquestionably the most picturesque and interesting of all the Negro strains in America is the Gullah. It is unique, in the real, true meaning of that much abused word."

Religious freedom was permitted—if not encouraged—in South Carolina from the very beginning, although the Church of England was established as the official state church in 1706. Today South Carolina can boast that only one other state has more church members in proportion to the total population.

One especially unique distinction in religion belongs to South Carolina. The Reformed branch of Judaism in America originated at Charleston in 1824 when the Reformed Society of Israelites was formed there. Charleston's first Jewish congregation was started in 1750.

Among the notable religious leaders, Bishop Francis Asbury, the "father of American Methodism," frequently toured the country preaching. He wrote, "I now leave Charleston, seat of Satan, dissipation and folly . . ." Of Georgetown, he wrote, "Here are the rich, the rice and the slaves; the last is awful to me." In the up-country he "met with a multitude of people who were desperately wicked."

However, he found the people generally kind and well-meaning and the countryside of great beauty.

Wilson's Snipe, *by John James Audubon. The background is thought to be a South Carolina plantation near Charleston, painted by Audubon's assistant, Swiss landscape artist George Lehmann.*

What would such a man think of South Carolina today? Would he feel that progress had been made? In spite of the many problems and injustices that still persist there, as well as in other states, the answer can hardly be anything but a resounding "Yes!"

Cypress Gardens near Charleston.

Natural Treasures

ANIMAL

"Why it's only a raccoon," said the visitor to Hilton Head Island in disappointment as the startled little animal with the sharp black eyes disappeared as quickly as it had appeared. "Don't be so sure," said his friend from the island. "I think it might have been our Hilton Head raccoon, and if it was, you have spotted one of the world's rarest animals. The Hilton Head Island raccoon is found only on this island in all the world."

Few South Carolina animals are in such a rare category, although the nearly extinct Carolina otter surely falls in that class. Of course, many of the animals that used to be plentiful in the state—puma, elk, bison—have completely disappeared. It comes as a surprise to many that buffalo once were plentiful so far east, since many people think of them only as animals of the western plains. The South Carolina town of Buffalo pays tribute to this truly American beast.

A number of animals have been introduced into the region, including the Asiatic monkeys of Hilton Head Island and Georgetown Neck. The marsh tacky were the small descendants of horses first brought by the Spanish in the 1500s. They are now gone.

The animals that remain range from the tiny shrew to an occasional wild hog, bear, and bobcat. Alligators may still be found in coastal and other damp regions.

A popular sport in South Carolina is "drag hunting." This is said "to have all the elements of fox hunting except the fox."

The sea fisherman has a choice of two-hundred-fifty species of ocean fish, including albacore, amberjack, angelfish, barracuda, bass, blackfish, bluefish, marlin, bonito, cubia, croaker, cutlass, dolphin, drum, grouper, ladyfish, mackerel, mullet, pugfish, pompano, rockfish, sailfish, sea bream, sea robin, shad, sheepshead, snapper, spadefish, spot, tarpon, tautog, triple tail, triggerfish, summer trout, tuna, wahoo, weakfish, whiting, and flounder. Gigging for flounder is one of the unusual and interesting sports.

The giant sea turtles of Fripp Island and other places, oysters, crab, clam, and shrimp have long added to South Carolina's wealth. The rare pygmy whale has been spotted on a few occasions.

Striped bass is the most famous freshwater game fish found in South Carolina. A fish with a local reputation but not so well known outside the state is the landlocked rockfish. There are 250 miles (402 kilometers) of trout fishing streams, where brown and rainbow trout wait for the lucky angler. Bream, shad, and other bass also are plentiful.

More than 360 species of birds are listed on the South Carolina records, including distant travelers from the Arctic regions as well as an occasional rare tropical visitor. The variety of birds is shown by the fact that there are said to be 250 types on Hilton Head Island alone.

To protect the wildlife of the state, there are such areas as Cape Romain National Refuge, a 35,000-acre (14,164 hectares) refuge near Charleston. Here ducks, plovers, and egrets brighten the gloomy swamps. The dignified great blue heron is known to the local people as "Po' Joe." They like to puzzle visitors with the question, "Did you ever see a fat 'Po' Joe' sittin' on a dead live oak stump, eatin' green blackberries and takin' a fresh salt water bath?"

One of the most thrilling sights in many South Carolina woodlands is to spot the elusive iridescent plumage of the great and beautiful wild turkey, a favorite since colonial days.

VEGETABLE

The palmetto (cabbage palm) has so worked its way into the affections of South Carolina people that they call the state the Palmetto State and proudly display this ornamental tree on their state flag.

However, other trees have more commercial value. In fact, the more than 12,000,000 acres (4,856,200 hectares) of forests are probably the single greatest natural resource in the state. After generations of use, forests still cover 61.7 percent of the total area of South Carolina. Evergreens spread over about 5,600,000 acres (2,266,240 hectares), and hardwoods blanket the balance.

To help protect the forests, the federal government has established two national forests—Francis Marion and Sumter—named in honor of two Revolutionary heroes of the state. Since 1927 billions of tree seedlings have been planted to keep the forests growing at the present annual rate of nearly 700,000,000 board feet.

One of the most interesting areas of the Sumter National Forest is the primeval growth of hemlock, with massive column-like trunks and arching limbs, giving a cathedral-like appearance to the area.

The more "exotic" trees of the state include the gorgeous evergreen holly, the olive, and cypress. A famous individual tree was the 1,000-year-old Angel Oak near Charleston.

Timber was so plentiful in early times that the "sapwood" was frequently thrown away and only the heart of a tree was used. Many "heart of pine" houses are still standing, and the wood is said to keep indefinitely.

Rhododendron and mountain laurel (Kalmia lafifolia) transform the forest trails into flower-lined corridors during the spring blooming season and blanket the mountain slopes. Cultivated plants such as the azalea are a spring tourist attraction in South Carolina.

Among the rarest plants are the gordonia and the strange Venus's-flytrap.

In such places as Bull Island the delightful scent of the beautiful state flower, yellow jessamine, is carried through the air; banana waterlily, widgeon grass, and the graceful sea oats add to the unique character of the scene.

The Indians used the evergreen leaves of the Jaupon or cassina holly to make a ceremonial drink, and cassina tea is still brewed. The shrub's waxy, brilliant red berries often help to keep the birds alive in seasons when the food supply is poor.

This is only one of the one hundred species of plants which have been found in just a 10-acre (4-hectare) region near Myrtle Beach.

MINERAL

Although some lead and gold have been mined in South Carolina, the state is not considered to have metallic or fuel minerals of commercial value.

However, from the famous blue-granite quarries near Winnsboro to the extraordinary glass sands (99 percent silica) of the Sand Hills, South Carolina's cache of minerals continues to hold out treasures for industry and science.

The native plastic clay, fine white kaolin clay, massive limestone formations of the Coastal Plain, silicones—raw materials of the Atomic Age—are only a few of the valuable minerals. Other minerals include barite, ilmenite, kyanite, zircon, marl, feldspar, sericite, foundry sand, monazite, gravel rutile, and mica.

Once scorned as useless is a mighty wonder known as vermiculite, of which South Carolina has vast stores.

The rocks of the state interest a growing number of rock hounds. Fossil and shell collecting in the Coastal Plain and on the South Carolina beaches is also increasingly popular. At many places in the state, particularly near McCormick, Kershaw, Jefferson, West Springs, Kings Creek, and Smyrna, panning for placer gold along the streams is a pleasant and sometimes rewarding hobby.

The freshwater supplies of South Carolina are listed as "virtually unlimited."

People Use Their Treasures

KEEPING THINGS SPINNING

The rapidly growing importance of manufacturing and the promise it holds of greater wealth for all the people probably represent the most dynamic activities in South Carolina today. Total value of the state's manufacturing is about six billion dollars per year.

South Carolina leads the world in production of cotton goods. Over a third of all the cotton spindles in the United States whir in South Carolina. The first cotton mill in America was built on James Island in 1789. One of the early promoters of cotton manufacture in South Carolina was Dr. John L.E.W. Shecut, who raised money by legal lottery to finance his Carolina Homespun Company in 1808. In that year the commons house of the state legislature forbade its members to appear in clothing other than Carolina homespun. Dr. Shecut named his daughter Carolina Homespun Shecut.

A billion and a half feet of saw timber is produced annually in South Carolina, but it is estimated the state's forests could support twice the present industry. There are hundreds of lumber mills and wood products plants. Furniture and woodwork factories produce products worth millions. Barrels, baskets, boxes, and veneering are imported.

The largest plant in the world for the manufacture of glass fibers operates at Aiken. Another of the mammoth manufacturers of the state is the Lockheed aviation plant at Charleston. Spring's cotton mills at Fort Mill is the world's largest plant for the manufacture of sheeting, and one of the largest Portland cement plants is that at Holly Hill.

Most impressive of all, perhaps, is the faith which large corporations have shown by their recent investments in South Carolina. The United States government has invested over a billion and a half dollars in the Atomic Energy installation near Aiken.

The nuclear power plants of Duke Power Company and Carolina Power and Light and the nuclear plant at Parr help to make South Carolina one of the leading states in generating atomic power.

Hartsville nuclear center.

Contrasted with these giant enterprises are such modest but interesting activities as the manufacture of candle wax from the local myrtle berries.

Another interesting business fact concerns the devotion of people to their jobs. The state claims the nation's "top records for least time lost through strikes, labor turnover, or absences."

"AND ON THAT FARM THEY RAISED ..."

Almost as soon as the colony had been started in 1670, an experimental farm was set up in the name of the lords proprietors to see what farm crops would do well. It was found that Madagascar rice would prosper in the swampy areas, and indigo for dyes could be a profitable crop. On his The Rocks Plantation, Peter Gaillard was the first to grow cotton successfully in South Carolina.

48

However, the state's leading crop was corn until 1850, when cotton took over. The state has always had the potential of corn leadership. In 1889 Frederick Drake of Bennettsville took the world's record with a production of 255 bushels (89.8 hectolitres) of corn per acre.

Great fortunes were built on cotton, rice, and indigo. Huge plantations sprawled over many acres, and were worked by large numbers of slaves. After 1865, many of these plantations fell into decay. Now sometimes all that is left is the avenue of drooping live oaks that once led to a prosperous and luxurious estate.

Today, some large plantations still exist, worked by hired labor with modern machinery. Some landowners still let out their acres on a sharecropping basis, while others rent. The backbone of the estate's farming today, however, is the independent farmer, raising an ever-widening variety of crops and depending more and more on livestock, poultry, and dairying.

Present farm income of the state is approaching one billion dollars per year. Tobacco has passed cotton in South Carolina, with the value of the cotton crop considerably lower. It is interesting to note that South Carolina farmers now plant more acres in soybeans than in cotton. Corn and hogs are next in value.

The leading cash crop, tobacco.

South Carolina ranks second among the states in the production of peaches—first in peaches for the fresh fruit market. Spartanburg calls itself the "fresh peach capital of the world." Within a 100-mile (161-kilometer) radius of Columbia there are about four million peach trees.

Apples, pears, and pecans are other leading orchard crops.

South Carolina has several agricultural "firsts." D.R. Williams was the first to use mules for agriculture in the southern states. David Coker introduced the use of pedigreed seed, and the first tea farm in America was at Summerville. The tomato was first cultivated in Oconee County.

To help sell agricultural products, South Carolina has established several State Farmers Markets.

LIGHTWEIGHT WONDER AND OTHERS

Only a few years ago anyone who mined vermiculite would have seemed more than a little odd. Yet today it is one of the minerals increasing most rapidly in demand. Not long ago it was found that concrete made with 30 pounds (13.6 kilograms) of vermiculite would be as strong as that using 400 pounds (181 kilograms) of sand and stone. Thirty pounds (13.6 kilograms) of vermiculite plaster will replace 150 pounds (68 kilograms) of sand plaster in a fireproof structural steel building. Use of this lightweight wonder saves millions and even billions of dollars in construction.

South Carolina's vast stores of vermiculite have brought the state second rank in vermiculite mining. The vermiculite plant near Lanford Station in Laurens County is the largest in the world.

South Carolina's plastic clay is being used in the manufacture of such varying products as bathtubs, pottery, automobile tires, and electrical outlets. The state's fine white kaolin clay is made into fine quality china, and also is used to give a slick surface to magazine paper.

The blue granite quarries near Winnsboro yield one of the country's most important building stones. A very superior grade of Portland cement can be obtained from the state's limestone formations. The especially high quality of silica sand is attracting glassmaking companies and manufacturers of silicones for paint, polishes, waxes, and cleaners. Along the riverbanks of the flood plains scientists find a number of minerals used in atomic production. Monazite contains thorium, used in nuclear reactors, and kyanite can stand extremely high temperatures. Corundum is used in grinding radar plates.

Even gold and tin have been mined in South Carolina. A small tin mine, among the few ever operated in this country, was opened in Cherokee County in 1937. The Haile gold mine near Kershaw has been worked occasionally since it was first started in 1828. In 1934 it was revived. Gold valued at $476,800 was produced in the state in 1939.

TRANSPORTATION AND COMMUNICATION

One of the first American-made steam locomotives, *The Best Friend of Charleston,* first operated in October, 1830, on a stretch of railroad out of Charleston. This was said to be the first railroad in the country to be designed for a steam engine.

According to the Charleston *Courier,* "The first trip was performed with two pleasure cars attached, and a small carriage, fitted for the occasion, upon which was a detachment of United States troops and a field piece which had been politely granted by Major Belton for the occasion." The cannon fired a salute at every stop; local beauties scattered flowers along the tracks in front of the train, and frightened spectators cowered as the puffing monster came near.

Before a year had passed, *The Best Friend* came to an unhappy finish. The fireman sat down on the safety valve when he could no longer stand the hiss of the steam. In the explosion that followed, the fireman was killed and the tiny engine destroyed. New ones soon replaced it, however.

By 1833 the South Carolina railroad had been extended for 136 miles (218.9 kilometers) to become the longest steam passenger railroad in the world at the time.

Water transportation, of course, was the first used in the region because it was the easiest. Passengers and freight made their way up and down the rivers. Almost every plantation had its own wharf, and many had their own boats. Dugout canoes called *pirogues,* propelled by slaves, sometimes carried as many as fifty passengers. Steamboats later provided quicker and more luxurious water transport.

Canals were begun to connect some of the major waterways or to bypass rapids and falls. The 22-mile (35-kilometer) Santee Canal was completed in 1800. Other canals were built at Dreher Shoals, Columbia, Lands Ford, and Rock Mount, but none of the canals was very successful for long.

Transportation was more difficult in the up-country where the rivers were shallow and fast. Early highways followed the Indian paths. Visitors frequently complained that the roads were among the worst they had ever seen. That situation is completely changed in modern South Carolina, with its thousands of miles of highways, including four highways of the huge interstate system.

It was the coming of the automobile, of course, that brought about the first real improvement in the roads. Great excitement in 1900 caused Columbia's newspaper *The State* to proclaim: "The first horseless carriage, a light automobile, made its appearance on the streets of Columbia yesterday. It was manipulated by two young men who had no difficulty in doing so. Many watched the machine with great interest. The running gear is light, but suited for the purpose. The machine is being taken about in the interest of a large soap manufacturing concern."

South Carolina has three major deepwater seaports—Charleston, Georgetown, and Port Royal. Port Royal Sound has the greatest natural depth of any harbor on the south Atlantic seaboard. In 1562, Jean Ribaut called it "One of the greatest and fairest havens in the world, where without danger all the ships in the world might be harboared." Georgetown has two marine terminals and Port Royal one.

The important Intracoastal Waterway also threads its course along the South Carolina coast.

Air travelers are served by over one hundred airports.

South Carolina's first newspaper was the Carolina *Gazette,* first

A cruise ship docked in Charleston.

published in 1732. The *Gazette* was owned in part by Benjamin Franklin and edited by his protégé, Lewis Timothee. His widow, Elizabeth Timothy (as she later spelled her name), edited the paper for some years after her husband died and was commended by Franklin for her business ability. She was the first-known woman in American journalism.

A portrait of John C. Calhoun by Arthur Conrad. Calhoun practiced law in South Carolina before he was elected to public office.

Human Treasures

THE PRESIDENT

A thirteen-year-old youngster who happened to be visiting his brother during the Revolutionary War Battle of Camden was captured by the British. He peered fiercely through the bars of the stockade jail to watch the rest of the fight. When a British officer commanded him to polish his boots, he refused. Not even the severe lashing with a saber, which left permanent scars, could cool the spirit of this young man, Andrew Jackson, who was as tough as native hickory.

Both North and South Carolina claim the birthplace of Andrew Jackson. With the border in its present position, it probably never will be possible to prove on which side the birth took place. It is likely that it may have been just over the South Carolina side of the boundary. Regardless of his birthplace, Jackson had many other associations with South Carolina both as a boy and man.

His father, Andrew, Sr., is buried in the Waxhaw Presbyterian cemetery near Lancaster. The story is told that when the elder Jackson died, his body was placed in a coffin on a sled and carried about from one place to another as the wake was being held. After the last stop, on the way to the cemetery, someone discovered that the body was no longer there. After some searching it was found where it had fallen into a snowbank, and it was then carried on to the burial place.

The dramatic and important events of Andrew Jackson's eventful life took place in other areas, but as president, Andrew Jackson had a head-on clash with his native state. The South Carolina convention of 1832 passed an Ordinance of Nullification, declaring that the tariff laws of 1828 were unconstitutional and therefore null and void.

Jackson gave his views on this action to a congressman from South Carolina who was about to return home from Washington: "Tell them," the president said, "that they can talk and write resolutions and print threats to their hearts' content. But if one drop of blood is shed there in defiance of the laws of the United States, I will hang the first man of them I can get my hands on, to the first tree I can find."

A South Carolina senator in talking to Missouri Senator Thomas Hart Benton said he doubted that Jackson would go so far. Benton had been one of Jackson's numerous dueling partners, and he warned, "When Jackson begins to talk about hanging, they can begin to look for the ropes."

THE STATESMAN

The principal opponent of President Jackson during most of his two terms in the White House was another South Carolina native, John Caldwell Calhoun, born in Abbeville County in what is known as the Long Cane region.

After becoming a lawyer, he began his political career in the South Carolina legislature, moved to the national Congress and then served as secretary of war. As John Calhoun rose steadily in experience and popularity, many, including Calhoun himself, felt that it was almost inevitable that some day he would be president.

Calhoun ran for the presidency in 1824, but was elected vice-president under John Quincy Adams. Once more he tried in 1828 and again only reached the vice-presidency, this time under Andrew Jackson. After increasing disputes with Jackson, Calhoun resigned to become a senator from South Carolina. Jackson turned his support to Van Buren and Calhoun never realized his ambition to be president. From this point on, Calhoun was recognized as the leader of the southern movement for stronger states and a less powerful federal government.

He remained in the Senate until 1844, when he became secretary of state under Tyler. He worked for the admission of the independent Republic of Texas as a state and finally brought this about.

Calhoun returned to the Senate where one of his major efforts was against the admission of California as a state where slavery was forbidden. He hinted that he would not give in on this point even though the Union might be broken.

At this time Henry Clay proposed a compromise that he hoped would satisfy both sides and admit California as well. Although Calhoun agreed with most of the compromise, he felt it did not give strong enough guarantees for the rights of the South. The meeting of the Senate on March 4, 1850, was one of the most unusual in the history of that body.

Calhoun had grown too old and weak to read his speech, but he had himself carried into the Senate chamber, and a friend read the old warrior's final plea for his beloved South, scorning the idea of compromise and insisting that what he felt were the injustices done to his region be corrected.

Within less than a month John Calhoun was dead; the compromise he fought was accepted, but he, himself, had never given in.

Only one South Carolina man, James J. Byrnes equaled John C. Calhoun in the number of prominent executive offices held. The record of both these outstanding South Carolina statesmen can be summarized and compared as follows: Calhoun—congressman, senator, secretary of war, secretary of state, twice vice president; Byrnes—senator, Supreme Court justice, director of economic stabilization, director of war mobilization, secretary of state, and governor of the state of South Carolina.

THE GENERAL: "ROBIN HOOD OF THE REVOLUTION"

Francis Marion was a modest, soft-spoken man "rather below middle stature, lean and swarthy," according to one of his followers. Forty-eight at the time the guerrilla action began, he always went into battle at the head of his forces, and his attacks were so fierce that he became the terror of the British troops.

Marion was a leader in whom his men had the greatest confidence. He never took unnecessary risks. He was wise and persistent, and always slept on the ground along with his men and shared their food.

Marion planned his attacks carefully, and his complete knowledge of the swampy wilderness where he operated was a great advantage.

He could advance and retreat over secret trails without any danger of being followed. He and his men learned and used such invaluable tricks as placing their blankets on bridges to muffle the clatter of horses' hooves which would warn the British of a coming attack.

Until he discharged his men in 1782 at Wadboo plantation, they never let up their pressure on the enemy.

Marion had been born in Berkeley County in 1732. He was not married when the war came, but he married his cousin after the war, and again took up the life of a planter on the Santee River. He died practically unnoticed at his plantation in February, 1795. Possibly his exploits would have been entirely lost to history if it had not been for Parson Weems and his fanciful stories, and yet few men have made a more useful or unusual contribution to their country.

HOW DOES YOUR GARDEN GROW?

In addition to its many magnificent gardens, South Carolina has two other claims to horticultural fame. Two of our best-known and most-admired flowers are named for South Carolina men.

Joel Robert Poinsett was one of the remarkable men of his time. Born wealthy, he was a most ardent supporter of democracy. One of the most traveled Americans of his day, he represented the United States in Chile, the first qualified agent of a foreign country in that nation. He served as a United States congressman and then was appointed minister to Mexico, returning to Washington as secretary of war. In Washington he became a leader of the intellectuals and served as first president of the National Institution for the Promotion of Science, which later became the Smithsonian Institution.

He was one of the founders of the Academy of Fine Arts at Charleston. He promoted the building of better roads and bridges throughout the state. He supported manufacturing with paid workers and was against slave labor.

Joel Poinsett brought home interesting plants and flowers of many places where he served throughout the world. One of these he introduced from Mexico, a plant with its topmost leaves turned

Many beautiful gardens, such as Magnolia Gardens near Charleston, can be seen throughout South Carolina.

scarlet. It soon became popular, and was named poinsettia in honor of the man who introduced it. Today almost every American probably speaks the name of Poinsett at least once during the Christmas season.

Dr. Alexander Garden was a Scottish physician who also loved flowers and plants and spent much time in cultivating them in his home near Beaufort. One of his specialties was a subtropical shrub sometimes known as cape jasmine. This flower, which was developed by Dr. Garden, now is known as the gardenia, in his honor.

OTHER PUBLIC FIGURES

A number of South Carolina families have provided several generations or many individuals of notable leadership. Charles Pinckney was a chief justice of the colony. His son, Charles Cotesworth Pinckney, was a soldier of the Revolution, a signer of the federal Constitution, a candidate for president, secretary of war and of state, and minister to France. He was one of the first to urge a strong state university. His brother Thomas was also a Revolutionary leader, governor of South Carolina, minister to England, and special emissary to Spain, who succeeded in opening the Mississippi

River to United States commerce. Their cousin, also a Charles Pinckney, was a delegate to the Constitutional Convention and author of a plan for the Constitution, which had many features that were written into the final document.

Richard I. Manning was the sixth member of the allied Richardson-Manning family to become a governor of South Carolina, a record probably not equaled in any other state. Mrs. Elizabeth Peyre Richardson Manning had the unusual distinction of being niece, wife, sister, mother, aunt, and grandmother of governors.

Another prominent family was the Hamptons. Wade Hampton III is probably South Carolina's favorite hero.

An "all-American" hero of the Revolution from South Carolina was William Moultrie, son of the Scottish physician Dr. Hugh Moultrie. William married an heiress at the age of eighteen and started life as a planter. Although he had been an officer of the crown, he went over to the Colonial side. His brilliant defense of Charleston was one of the turning points in the Revolution. If the colonies had lost Charleston then, the South would probably have fallen, and it is likely that the Revolution would have been lost. He was captured when the British finally took Charleston in 1780 and was their prisoner for two years. He was later a governor of the state and his published *Memoirs of the Revolution* are well known.

Another Revolutionary hero was General Andrew Pickens, who became renowned as an Indian fighter. He won his final victory over the Cherokee as late as 1799. He was surrounded by the Indian forces with little chance of escape, until he set the nearby bamboo canebreak on fire. The joints of the bamboo exploded like guns; the Indians thought reinforcements had come, and they hurried away, according to tradition.

In Pickens' later years the Indians came to respect him so much that they called him *Skyagusta* (Wizard Owl) and brought him many gifts. He died in 1817 at his home, the Red House, near Walhalla.

Thomas Sumter was born in Virginia, but he operated a plantation on the Santee River. Like General Marion, General Sumter gathered a group of South Carolina men for guerrilla activity against the British. Some had only pitchforks for weapons, and they had few if any uniforms, but they were so sprightly in their harassing attacks that Cornwallis nicknamed Sumter the Gamecock.

Henry Laurens of Mepkin Estate gained fame as president of the Continental Congress. Captured by the British, he was held in the Tower of London. He was given his release in exchange for America's most famous war prisoner—Lord Cornwallis. Laurens insisted that when he died his body be cremated so that he would not be buried alive. This is considered to be the first cremation in American history.

Laurens' son, John, was sent to France to get aid for the Revolutionary cause. When he could not see the king, he brushed aside the rules and approached the monarch at a party, finally getting a promise of help. John Laurens was killed in the war at the age of twenty-eight. George Washington lamented his death, "He had no fault that I could discover—unless it were an intrepidity bordering on rashness."

General Richard H. (Fighting Dick) Anderson was the highest ranking South Carolina officer of the Confederacy. Other Confederate generals included Stephen D. Lee, James Longstreet, and Daniel H. Hill, along with seven other generals of lesser rank.

Johnson Hagood was another who served both as general and governor. In later years when someone asked him which title he preferred, he replied, "Call me General; I fought for that and begged for the other."

An outstanding leader of the Spanish-American War, Admiral Victor Blue, lived his boyhood years at Marion on the family plantation, Bluefields. He received a citation for "extraordinary heroism" during the war with Spain.

Joseph Alston, governor from 1812 to 1814, is remembered particularly as the husband of Theodosia Burr, daughter of Aaron Burr and one of the best-known women of her time. In 1812 she left their plantation, The Oaks, and sailed on the schooner *Patriot* from the port of Georgetown to visit her notorious father in New York. For weeks the father paced the New York pier, but nothing more was ever heard of the ship or its famous passenger.

A strange story was told by an old man on his death bed. He claimed to have been a member of a pirate crew that had captured the *Patriot* and its passengers. The beautiful Theodosia was sentenced to walk the plank, and it was his lot to turn the plank and send her into the sea. She appeared on deck ready for her execution, he said, dressed all in white and carrying a white Bible. As she sank into the sea her long hair floated for a moment in a froth of foam.

The true fate of Theodosia Burr is one of the intriguing mysteries of history.

SUCH INGENIOUS PEOPLE

Noted as both a scientist and governor was David Rogerson Williams, a general of the War of 1812, who was elected governor by the legislature, supposedly without his knowledge. He discovered a method of illuminating his house with wood gas, found a method of obtaining oil from cottonseed, and brought about many advancements in cotton and rope production.

Dr. Francis L. Parker was one of South Carolina's many notable medical leaders. He was the first surgeon ever to suture a divided nerve. Dr. J. Marion Sims gained a reputation as the "Father of Gynecology." Dr. Mathilda Evans is known as the first black woman to found a hospital.

The Reverend John Leighton Wilson has an unusual claim to fame. As a missionary in Africa he became an authority on the animals there and is credited as the discoverer of the gorilla, his most outstanding accomplishment.

John Pratt was the inventor of a typewriter, and probably should be credited with the first typewriter. However, he was about two weeks late in filing for his patent. Solomon Jones is hailed by many as having been "America's first builder of scenic roads." David Coker's experiments resulted in cotton with a longer staple, an improved type of seed corn, and many other things.

Henry William Ravenel was an internationally known botanist. One of his collections was bought by the British Museum and may still be seen there. More names in mycology (fungus) bear his name as discoverer than that of any other botanist.

One of America's earliest scientists was Dr. Henry Woodward, the first English settler in South Carolina, a real student of the animals and plants of the region. Captured by the Spanish, he was taken to the East Indies. Returning to South Carolina, he introduced Madagascar rice. He made friends with the Indians for miles around and helped them with their problems. Without his skill and knowledge the first colony might not have survived. He fell ill on a visit to the Indians, who faithfully carried him back to Charles Towne, but he died before they could reach it, and the Indians buried him in an unknown grave.

SUCH CREATIVE PEOPLE

In literature, Henry Timrod long was known as the "unofficial poet laureate of the South." His fortune was wiped out in the Reconstruction period, and he was forced to sell his possessions but did not lose his spirit. He wrote figuratively to a friend, "We have eaten two silver pitchers, one or two dozen forks, several sofas, innumerable chairs, and a huge bedstead."

Whenever a chairman calls a meeting to order, Henry Martin Roberts of Robertsville, who served as a Union soldier, is remembered. He created the universally used *Roberts Rules of Order*. He was also a noted specialist in military engineering.

Elliott White Springs gained fame as a World War I flying ace. As an author, his satires on the war gained a large readership. He startled the townspeople of Lancaster by stunting over his father's mills there. Finally he took over the operation of the business, which he vastly increased.

Julia Peterkin of Fort Motte won the 1928 Pulitzer Prize for her grim and realistic novel *Scarlet Sister Mary*.

J. Gordon Coogler gained a reverse kind of fame because some of his poems were so bad they brought the word Cooglerism into the language, meaning a kind of absurd poetry. William Gilmore Simms was the author of eighty books; of these, twenty-four volumes were poetry.

Another poet, novelist, and dramatist was DuBose Heyward, who wrote *Porgy,* the work on which Gershwin's opera *Porgy and Bess* was based. George Gershwin himself spent a number of months on the South Carolina coast, absorbing the atmosphere of the region before tackling the work that gave him great fame.

The best-known composer of South Carolina was Lily Strickland from Anderson whose Oriental songs and songs of the South gained a wide following. Her *Honey Chile* and *Lindy Lou* are still sung.

Robert Mills, native of Charleston, gained renown as the first federal architect. He designed many prominent homes and public buildings in South Carolina and is probably best known as the architect of the Washington Monument and the United States Treasury Building in Washington, D.C.

Clark Mills of Charleston was a cabinetmaker and self-taught sculptor. Although he had never seen an equestrian statue before, he accepted a commission by Congress to make a statue of Andrew Jackson on his horse. After several years he managed this difficult task, and this work, now in Washington, was the first equestrian statue ever made in this country.

Henrietta Johnson is considered to be "America's first woman artist." Recent artists of more than local fame include Elizabeth O'Neill Verner and Alice R.H. Smith.

SUCH INTERESTING PEOPLE

Many South Carolina people are noted for their work for their fellowman. The Reverend Charles Jaggers, of Columbia, former slave, founded the Jaggers Old Folks' Home for Negroes. He preached for seventy-nine years from one text: "Let this mind be in you which was also in Christ Jesus." On his death, the governor attended his funeral and all business houses of Columbia closed by proclamation of the mayor.

The Reverend Daniel J. Jenkins founded the Jenkins Institute for

64

destitute black children and kept it going personally as long as he was able. Later, to help support the orphanage, the institute's band played benefit concerts as far away as Canada and Europe.

The Reverend William Plumer Jacobs, founder of Clinton, created the community almost single-handedly. He solicited more than a million dollars for the support of the orphans of Thornwell Orphanage and founded Presbyterian College at Clinton.

Willie Lee Buffington never forgot the encouragement he had received from Eury Simkins, a black teacher. Although he had no money, Buffington founded a well-known library for blacks, as he said, on "faith and a dime."

Ann Pamela Cunningham, although a lifetime invalid, was a principal organizer of the Mount Vernon Ladies Association that saved George Washington's home as a shrine.

A Revolutionary heroine was Jane Thomas of Clifton who swam her horse across Hurricane Shoals to warn the patriots of a coming British attack. A Reconstruction heroine was Andrea Dorothea Olga Siva Lucy Holcombe Douschka Francesca Pickens, who is said to have recruited fifteen hundred men to follow General Hampton's Red Shirts.

A Reconstruction heroine was Manse Jolly of Anderson, who defied all the federal troops, refused to surrender, and was granted amnesty by the frightened Union colonel. On the other side was Robert Smalls, member of a Confederate crew of slaves; he captured the Confederate ship *Planter* and brought it to Union officials. He later was elected to a seat in Congress and was able to buy the estate of his former "owner."

Marie Boozer was denounced by her fellow Columbians when she rode in a carriage with Northern officers in their victory parade in the capital. She married a Union officer, later became friendly with members of the court of Napoleon III of France and married a French count. They went to China, where she then married a nobleman from Japan, who is said to have had her beheaded.

Melvin Purvis was born at Timmonsville. This FBI man trapped the notorious gangster Dillinger, and a popular television show was based on his life.

McKissic Library at the University of South Carolina.

Teaching and Learning

In South Carolina today there are more than twenty colleges and universities.

Founded at Columbia in 1801 as South Carolina College, the institution now known as the University of South Carolina claims to be the first educational institution in the country entirely supported by state funds. Early distinctions were the establishment at the university in 1840 of the first chair of political science in the United States, and the first separate college library in the United States.

After Reconstruction, the university was closed in 1877 and reopened in 1880. It now enrolls over twenty thousand students. Among the other state-supported institutions are Winthrop College in Rock Hill, South Carolina State College in Orangeburg, The Citadel in Charleston, and Clemson University in Clemson.

The Citadel took its name from the Charleston fortress in which the first classes were held. The school moved to its present campus in 1922. It gained additional fame when renowned World War II General Mark Clark became its president. It is proud both of its unique military history and its reputation as a "fortress of learning."

Clemson is the state college of agriculture and mechanic arts. Thomas G. Clemson, John C. Calhoun's son-in-law, left most of his estate to ". . . an Agricultural College, which will afford useful information to the farmers and mechanics." Clemson operates the country's largest school of textile engineering, and is noted for its unique ceramics research department.

Opened in 1790, the College of Charleston is considered by many authorities to be the earliest municipal college in the United States. The Medical University of South Carolina in Charleston was founded in 1824 and was the first medical school founded in the state. In 1913 it became state operated.

A Methodist minister of Spartanburg, the Reverend Benjamin Wofford, left an estate of one hundred thousand dollars for "the founding of a college in my native district." At the time, 1850, this was the largest amount ever willed to a southern college. The institution today, of course, is Wofford College in Spartanburg.

The Citadel, in Charleston, was founded in 1842 as a military college. Classes were first held in the fortress in Charleston.

The rolls of South Carolina colleges include Erskine, Due West; Presbyterian, Clinton; Newberry, Newberry; Benedict College and Columbia College at Columbia; and Claflin College, Orangeburg.

South Carolina made notable progress in public education following World War II, spending millions on new school construction. The entire income from the state's retail sales tax must be used for education. This continues a tradition of public education that began in 1722 with an enactment for free schools. There are more children of school age in South Carolina in proportion to the population than in any other state.

One of the country's pioneering programs in public education was begun at the Parker District School near Greenville in 1923. Classes were converted to workshops, and teachers developed their own mimeographed textbooks. The school owned its own camp for school camping projects. The school was made the focus of activities for a large community. Many parts of the program have since been adopted by other schools across the country.

In 1918 the state department of education created what has been called "one of the most unique adult education programs in the nation." It concentrated on teaching adults to read and helped greatly in reducing the number of citizens who could not read. Dr. Wil Lou Gray was the remarkable leader of this movement.

A program of technical training begun by the state in 1961 has "proved truly amazing in its success." It operates technical training centers throughout the state with full technical curricula as well as training programs designed to meet the needs of specific industries. Many major firms have taken advantage of the program and have located large plants in the state because of it. It is estimated that the superior craftsmanship now found in South Carolina can make a machine in fifty-six minutes, while it would take eighty-four minutes in some other states. In one plant the labor force was trained in half the time estimated.

Among South Carolina's many leading educators have been Mary McLeod Bethune, native of Mayesville; Dr. James H. Carlisle, president of Wofford for fifty-four years; and Dr. Moses Waddell, noted pioneer educator.

The state's many achievements in other fields of education include the founding at Charleston of what is called the "first library in the country ever set up with public funds."

A view of Charleston from the air.

Enchantment of South Carolina

"UNLIKE ANY OTHERS"

Nature has provided South Carolina with everything needed to explode into colorful bloom each spring. With this natural advantage it is not surprising that the gardens of the state have a reputation for being the finest in the country. As DuBose Heyward said, South Carolina gardens ". . . blended ordered lines with natural beauty . . . grew and mellowed into gardens unlike any others in the whole world."

Almost from the beginning South Carolinians have gathered around them the floral beauty from the whole earth, and their unusual creations have been jealously guarded and improved ever since—"each step a breathtaking delight, each month a rush of new life. . ."

And yet these garden showplaces are only part of the attraction of South Carolina. In the state where luxury and comfort first found a foothold in America, there are reminders of the glorious past in hundreds of historical shrines, forts, public buildings, museums, mansions, and churches.

In addition, forty state parks help to preserve the scenic beauties of the state, in a sweep from seashore to mountains.

These and a multitude of other attractions now bring millions of tourists to South Carolina each year, and the money they spend makes tourism one of the important businesses of the state.

"CULTURAL CENTER OF THE NEW WORLD," CHARLESTON

Charleston has gathered an impressive list of American "firsts": first performance of a named opera, first American Shakespeare performance, first public museum in the country, first symphony orchestra in the nation, first musical society in America, the world's first department store, the first chamber of commerce in the country, first government supported public library, first seaside boardwalk in the nation, originator of the Big Apple and Charleston dances, and even of a drink called the Planters Punch, from the hotel where it was first served.

Charleston early became noted as a center of wealth and ease. Its people liked the good life and knew how to live it. They turned their attention early to art, music, and recreation. It is not surprising that Charleston gained the reputation as the center of luxury of the colonies. As an example of the eagerness with which they took to new uses of leisure time is the fact that as early as 1791 Charleston already had two golf courses.

Wealthy Charleston people were theater minded. Picturesque old Dock Street Theater is claimed as the first true theater in the nation. It was built in 1736 and later was partly destroyed by fire. Then the famed old Planters Hotel was built around it. Today the quaint old theater building has been completely restored so that visitors may make an excursion into the theatrical past as well as see a modern performance there.

America's first museum was founded in Charleston and is still operating today. The Charleston Museum, founded in 1773, is the largest in the city. Although its emphasis is on South Carolina material, it has collections of natural history from all over the world. The Gibbes Art Gallery, donated by James S. Gibbes, is housed in this building.

The St. Cecilia Society, begun in 1762, is probably the first musical society established in the United States. Today the society holds annual balls, and many people of Charleston would prefer the honor of an invitation to the St. Cecilia ball to presentation at court in England.

From its beginning in 1670 Charleston has been a most unusual city. It has survived plagues, pirates, wars (beginning with the Indian wars), five great fires, earthquakes, and many mighty hurricanes while continuing to maintain its reputation as the most "comfortable and luxurious" of cities.

One of the most trying periods of its history occurred when the pirate Blackbeard grew so strong and arrogant that he blockaded Charleston harbor and threatened to burn the city. Another

*Visitors can capture the charm of colonial
and pre-Civil War days in Charleston.*

notorious pirate of the period, a woman, came from the Charleston area. This was the beautiful and ruthless Ann Bonney.

Only memories of the pirates remain, of course; these memories are particularly strong in Whitepoint Gardens where Bonnet, Worley, and so many others were hanged. But so much else of the old Charleston is still on view that one authority declares, "It is far more beautiful, interesting, quaint, and charming than the French quarter of New Orleans or any other American city."

Especially interesting is St. Philip's Church. From its steeple gleamed a navigation light to aid Confederate ships, but it escaped Union cannon fire. John Calhoun is buried with other notables in St. Philip's cemetery.

The four clock faces in the steeple of St. Michael's Church (1752) have provided the time for the people of Charleston since 1764. The bells in the steeple have crossed the Atlantic five times, mostly for repairs. St. Michael's churchyard includes among other points of interest the grave of Mary Layton, who could not afford a tombstone, and the grave was marked with her cypress bedstead which lasted over a hundred years.

Other interesting houses of worship include St. Mary's, Unitarian; St. John's, French Huguenot; and the synagogue of Kahal Kadosh Beth Elohim congregation.

Many visitors are charmed by the narrow side lanes and alleys that lead to quiet courts and interesting homes.

Of the many old houses still standing, the most picturesque are huddled together and painted in such bright colors that they are known as Rainbow Row. The Nathaniel Russell House with its "astonishing flying stairs," Haywood-Washington House, Joseph Manigault Mansion, and Edmunsbon-Alston House are among the best-known houses of the city. Much of the work of maintaining and restoring Charleston is being carried on by the Historic Charleston Foundation. The city, in trying to keep its older structures rather than tear them down, has developed what it calls "Area Rehabilitation."

City Hall has a wonderful picture gallery. During the years, artists were commissioned to paint the portraits of visiting notables.

Included among the paintings still on display here is a portrait of George Washington in later years, in which he was shown not wearing his wig or false teeth.

Wrought iron and cast iron decorative work in pillars, railings, and fences is everywhere. There are so many fine iron gates that it is known as the "City of Famous Gateways." One of these guards the Sword Gate House, which takes its name from the wrought iron spears that join at the gate's center.

Charleston has renovated the old Provost Dungeon in the basement of the old Exchange Building, where British tea was hidden,

The old Exchange Building in Charleston.

where delegates to the Continental Congress were elected, where General Moultrie successfully hid ten thousand pounds (4,536 kilograms) of powder from the British, and where the British held American war prisoners. Here also may be seen a section of the old wall of the city. Charleston was one of the two walled cities of the United States. The National Society of Colonial Dames operates a museum of history in this building. Other Charleston museums include Confederate Museum in the old Market Hall and Old Slave Mart Museum and Gallery.

The Charleston waterfront holds much of interest. The Cooper and Ashley rivers were named in honor of Anthony Ashley Cooper, one of the principal proprietors. Historic old Fort Sumter National Monument may be visited. Admiral Farragut's flagship *Hartford* was

An aerial view of Fort Sumter.

given to the United States Navy Yard at Charleston, the only such yard south of Norfolk on the Atlantic Coast. At old Fort Moultrie is the grave of one of America's most noted Indian leaders—Chief Osceola, who died as a prisoner there. Nearby, a memorial is dedicated to the sixty-six crewmen of the Federal Ship *Patapsco,* the first ever to be torpedoed and sunk during wartime.

One of the most striking features of the waterfront is the very high John P. Grace Memorial Bridge arching across to the east shore. Another waterfront attraction is the city's marina, adding to the ease and comfort of boaters.

CHARLESTON'S "RIOT OF BLOOM"

Three of the world's best-known gardens are found in the Charleston area: Cypress, Magnolia, and Middleton Place.

President of the Continental Congress Henry Middleton knew many of the gardens of Europe from personal visits and study. He conceived the idea to create on his estate America's first landscaped garden and make it a showplace of the world.

In 1741 he put one hundred men to work laying out and molding the broad sweeping terraces that even today are not equaled anywhere else. They labored for ten years before the butterfly pools, formal walks, and other features were completed. Arthur Middleton, son of Henry, continued his father's work and employed Michaux, a famed botanist, who brought to Middleton the first camellias to be planted in America. Today at Middleton Place Gardens three of the four camellia plants he brought are still flourishing—large as trees.

Sixty years ago the *Baedeker Guide,* standard guidebook to world tourist attractions, listed only three two-star tourist points in the United States: Niagara Falls, the Grand Canyon, and Magnolia Gardens. Many feel that Magnolia Gardens still deserves to be ranked with the country's top attractions. British author John Galsworthy wrote, "I specialize in gardens, and freely assert that none other in the world is so beautiful. It is a kind of paradise which has wandered

Middleton Gardens, near Charleston, are one of the oldest landscaped gardens in the country.

down, a miraculously enchanted wilderness." This garden has been continuously owned by the Drayton family since 1671.

Visitors to Cypress Gardens are poled across the onyx-black waters in small boats, wandering through the narrow spaces between the hundreds of ancient cypress trees that grow straight and tall from the water. On every bank and island color blazes from azaleas, camellias, daffodils, and others and they are mirrored in the black waters. Many visitors, as they paddle along through the engulfed forest, have said they have the feeling of being "out of this world." Paths wander along banks and islands, connected by rose-festooned bridges. This garden once was a reservoir for the rice fields of Dean Hall Plantation; it was transformed into a showplace of nature and opened in 1930.

THE REST OF THE LOW-COUNTRY

Pleasures of the South Carolina shore range from the attraction of remote, almost uninhabited islands of Beaufort County to the many sophisticated resorts along the coast.

Hilton Head, a secluded resort island, has everything from a host of wildlife to two 18-hole golf courses. Edisto Island is noted for famous plantation homes, former slave quarters with their "lucky" blue shutters, and formal estate gardens.

Bull Island, rich in history, is a remote nature-lover's island, part of the Cape Romain National Refuge. Here bald eagles, horned grebes, gadwalls, coots, dowitchers, plovers, snowy egrets, and other creatures abound.

Pawleys Island, "where even bank presidents go barefoot," is home of the woven-rope hammock—and of the legend of the friendly Gray-Man ghost, who warns the people of coming storms. Some say the bellowing of a bull alligator is an even better warning of bad weather.

Founded in 1711, Beaufort is South Carolina's second oldest community, and it still preserves the charm of early days. The interesting and eccentric collection of things at the Beaufort Museum and other

A water festival is held in Beaufort every July.

sights may be seen in a walking tour of the city. One of these sights is famous St. Helena's Church. The silver communion set, still used by the church, was given by John Bull in memory of his wife, who was carried off by Indians.

The noted harbor was the scene of an amusing incident. Jones, a planter, had long tried to discover perpetual motion. One day his boat was seen to be dashing about the harbor without any visible means of locomotion. The cry went up that Jones had really found perpetual motion. Many came to watch and marvel. Later it was found that he had speared a large sting ray, and the creature towed him out to sea before he could cut the line.

Historic Parris Island was the site of the French settlement of 1562. Since 1915 it has been the principal Marine recruiting and training depot.

At Georgetown, named for the Prince of Wales who became George II, Prince George Winyah Church was built with brick brought from England as ballast in ships. It was used as a British stable during the Revolution, and hoof marks from that time may still be seen.

Also at Georgetown is the mouth of the Pee Dee River. Stephen Foster had chosen this for his famous song, until he changed it to the Suwanee River in Florida. Fort White, Belle Island Gardens, and Brookgreen Gardens are other attractions of the Georgetown region. Brookgreen has the oldest cultivated live oaks in America, and its collection of marble and bronze sculpture is spectacular.

Near Pineville is the grave of Francis Marion, Swamp Fox hero of the Revolution.

Myrtle Beach is the metropolis of 50 miles (80 kilometers) of beach communities known as the Grand Strand. In Florence, Sumter, and Clarendon counties are found some of the country's strangest natural features—the Carolina Bays. From the air these appear to be saucers of various sizes hollowed out of the earth. It was once thought they were made by a shower of metors, but many doubt this theory, and no one knows what they are or how they came to be. The area is now Woods Bay State Park.

THE CAPITAL

Columbia was created because the up-country farmers felt they could never have a just share in the government as long as the capital remained Charleston. So the new planned capital with its broad boulevards was founded in the center of the state in 1786.

Although the city was burned in 1865 during the Civil War, many old houses were saved. Almost every building left from that period has its special tale of how it escaped the fire.

Trinity Episcopal Church was built in 1846. During the war, lead from its roof was melted down for bullets. Three of the Wade Hamptons of that prominent family are buried in its churchyard.

The statehouse is one of the loveliest and most graceful in the nation, also one of the unluckiest. The beginning construction work was faulty, and in 1854 a new architect had to tear most of it down and begin again. It was unfinished when Sherman shelled the city in 1865, and scars of the shells that struck may still be seen. It was first used in 1869 and finished in 1907.

A poetic description of the statehouse says that visitors may "Stand in the marbled lobby . . . and gaze upward at the great stained-glass seal that spills its colors at their feet . . . Pass on the wrought-iron stairways the signers of the Declaration and Constitution . . . Meet in marbled halls John C. Calhoun . . . Hampton . . . Sumter . . . Marion . . . Pickens . . . Hear the guns of her six great wars . . . the muffled tread of her dead . . . all enshrined in a building so beautiful even Sherman spared it. . . ."

On the grounds one of the most unusual sculptures is the iron palmetto tree, in memory of the Palmetto Regiment of the war with Mexico. Other memorials and monuments dot the grounds.

The governor's mansion was originally built as the officers' quarters for an arsenal and is the only building left by Union troops on the arsenal grounds.

An important event in Columbia's calendar is the State Fair, held every October, which began in 1856.

Near Columbia are the stables of the Buxton Brothers, where such world-renowned horses as Sea Biscuit, Bold Venture, Cavalcade, and others were trained.

The boyhood home of Woodrow Wilson at Columbia has been turned into a museum.

Beautiful restorations are Ainsley Hall Mansion and Hampton-Preston House. Ainsley is a very fine example of Robert Mills' architecture. A fine collection of art is housed in the Columbia Museum of Art and Science.

In Columbia visitors may tour the campuses of the University of South Carolina, Benedict College, and Columbia College.

Cayce and West Columbia are thriving suburbs.

82

The state capitol, called the State House, in Columbia.

THE REST OF THE MIDDLE COUNTRY

Aiken is one of the country's most fashionable resorts, surrounded by the luxurious estates of wealthy people, mostly from out of state. It calls itself the Polo Capital of the South. When polo was introduced in 1882, a Charleston newspaper noted that: "It caused a great sensation and completely revolutionized the city as far as amusements are concerned." Farm club work by Mrs. Marie Siegler at Aiken was later expanded into the National 4-H movement.

Edgefield is known as the home of nine governors and five lieutenant governors. Near Edgefield was born Congressman Preston S. Brooks, who gained notoriety by caning Senator Charles Sumner from Massachusetts in an argument over slavery.

To create the vast Savannah River Plant of the Atomic Energy Commission, seven towns and six thousand persons had to be moved out of the area, which now is known as the birthplace of the hydrogen bomb.

Orangeburg is the site of Edisto Gardens with its curious Chinese waterwheel. At Fort Motte the bravery of Rebecca Motte is still remembered. The British had seized her home there to be used as their headquarters. During the Battle of Fort Motte, she brought out fire arrows which she stored away and called on the Americans to set her home afire. The British soon surrendered and American men quickly pulled out the burning arrows and put out the blaze.

Sumter is the home of Swan Lake Iris Gardens, one of the largest collection of irises in the country. Shaw Air Force Base and Scotts Lake Indian Mound are near Sumter. At Stateburg is the grave of General Sumter and a monument to him.

The oldest inland town in the state is Camden, proud of its record as the birthplace region of six Confederate generals. Famous advisor to many presidents, Bernard Baruch, was also a native of Camden. Baron de Kalb, German hero of the Revolution, died at the Battle of Camden, and a monument was made to him there. Another monument is the unique weather vane of the City Hall tower, honoring Chief Haigler of the Catawba, a friend of the Quaker settlers.

Near Bishopville the last duel in South Carolina was fought. This brought about a state law against dueling, and even today state officers must take an oath that they will not engage in dueling.

Winnsboro once was forced to mortgage the town clock to gain funds. The lender had to foreclose, but not having any use for the clock he finally gave it back.

Marion is named for the Revolutionary general. The story is told that after the Battle of Blue Savanna some of Marion's men found a dead British soldier who had not been shot. They found a rattlesnake and decided to court martial the snake for the soldier's death. The snake's attorney argued, "If this creature is a murderer, then so are we all. This snake has killed one British soldier; we have killed many. This is not murder, gentlemen. This is war." The soldiers shouted, "Not guilty," and the snake crawled away a free reptile.

Mullins is sometimes called the "Tobacco Capital of South Carolina."

A quaint story about Cheraw concerns St. David's Church, used as a hospital in the Revolution. Both the Presbyterians and the Baptists wanted to take over the old building for use as a church again. The Baptists managed to get inside; the Presbyterians fired an old cannon at the building, and the Baptists hurried out. At this point the

Episcopalians took over, and the Presbyterian minister wrote, "While the lion and the unicorn were fighting for the crown, up came the puppy dog and knocked them both down."

THE UP-COUNTRY

Spartanburg and Greenville, vigorous leaders of the Piedmont country, are almost close enough together to form a continuous metropolis of the highlands, and someday the two cities may be joined. The textile mills and other plants of the region make it the industrial hub of South Carolina. Greenville celebrates this leadership with the Southern Textile Exposition each year.

Near Greenville is Paris Mountain State Park. Spartanburg takes its name from the Spartan Regiment of South Carolina; these were the militiamen who became heroes of the Battle of the Cowpens. At Spartanburg is a monument to General Morgan, American victor at Cowpens.

Spartanburg has long been a transportation center. The interesting old Foster's Tavern was a favorite stopping place for travelers on the road between Georgia and Virginia.

When the first railroad arrived, thousands of people came from the entire region to celebrate with 8,000 pounds (3,629 kilograms) of barbecued meat in addition to speech making and toasts.

Cowpens National Battlefield Military Site is near Gaffney, and the Battle of Kings Mountain is remembered in Kings Mountain National Military Park. At the latter, there is a museum and administration building, and the mountain crest battleground is well marked for those who take the walking tour to see the positions once held by the troops.

Near Clover lived T.M. Thomas, aged nine, and his brother Paul, six. They wanted to buy a calf but did not have the money, so they invested their five dollars in turkeys. This was the beginning of one of the country's large turkey ranches.

At Rock Hill is the Children's Nature Museum of York County. Nearby is Andrew Jackson Historical State Park, supposed to be the

Kings Mountain National Military Park.

location of his birth. Also near Rock Hill is the Catawba Indian Reservation, last home of an Indian group in the state.

Among the natural features of the mountain country are spectacular Whitewater Falls in Oconee County and Table Rock, the legendary giant dining table of an Indian chief.

Anderson was named for Revolutionary hero General Robert Anderson. It was the first town in the South to have an almost unlimited supply of hydroelectric power, due to the generating plant at High Shoals on the Rocky River, built in 1894 by W.C. Whitner. The first cotton gin in the world to be operated by electricity was that of Oliver Bolt in Anderson County in 1897.

In front of the Anderson County Courthouse in Anderson is "The Old Reformer," a cannon used by both the British and Americans in the Revolution. It fired a triumphant signal in 1860 when the Secession Ordinance was signed. The Farmers Society Building is considered to be the first of its kind in America.

Near Anderson is Hartwell Dam and Reservoir of 62,000 acres (25,090 hectares), with a 962-mile (1,548-kilometer) shoreline.

Andrew Johnson, who became president on the death of Lincoln, had his tailor shop at Laurens. He gained great favor with the ladies by helping them with their quilting patterns and stitches.

The state bird, the Carolina wren, and state flower, the Carolina jessamine.

Woodward was the scene of a strange event, probably a legend. General Pakenham, British leader at the Battle of New Orleans in 1814, was killed in the fight and his body embalmed in a keg of rum to be shipped home to England. By accident the keg was sent to Woodward. The story is told that the keg was tapped frequently for drinks but did not seem to get any lighter. Finally it was broken open and the body found. Little drinking was done in the region for a long time after this.

Fountain Inn was the birthplace of Clayton "Peg Leg" Bates, who refused to be stopped by the loss of his leg and became a well-known dancer and theatrical figure.

His courage and determination are typical of the state itself, which, undismayed by troubles of every kind over the years, has won its way back to new peaks of accomplishment in the present day.

HANDY REFERENCE SECTION

Instant Facts

Became the 8th state, May 23, 1788
Capital—Columbia, founded 1786
Nickname—The Palmetto State
State mottoes—*Animis opibusque parate* (Prepared in mind and resources) and
        Dum spiro spero (While I breathe, I hope)
State bird—Carolina wren
State fish—Striped bass
State tree—Palmetto *(Sabal palmetto)*
State flower—Carolina jessamine (Yellow jessamine)
State stone—Blue granite
State symbol—The state sword
State song—"Carolina," words by Henry Timrod, music by Anne Custin Burgess
Area—31,055 square miles (80,432 square kilometers)
Rank in area—40th
Coastline—187 miles (301 kilometers)
Shoreline—2,876 miles (4,628 kilometers)
Greatest length (north to south)—210 miles (338 kilometers)
Greatest width (east to west)—273 miles (439 kilometers)
Geographic center—13 miles (20.9 kilometers) southeast of Columbia
Highest point—3,560 feet (1,085 meters), Sassafras Mountain
Lowest point—Sea level
Mean elevation—350 feet (107 meters)
Number of counties—46
Population—2,731,000 (1980 projection)
Rank in population—26th
Population density—83 persons per square mile (32 persons per square
        kilometer), 1970 census
Population center—In Richmond County, 4.5 miles (7.2 kilometers) north of
        Columbia
Illiteracy rate—2.3 percent
Birthrate—18.0 per 1,000
Infant mortality rate—23 per 1,000 births
Physicians per 100,000—108

Principal cities—	Columbia	113,542 (1970 census)
	Charleston	66,945
	Greenville	61,436
	Spartanburg	44,546
	Anderson	27,556
	Florence	25,997

You Have a Date with History

1526—First settlement, by Ayllón
1540-41—De Soto explores
1562—First Protestant settlement in America
1670—Charles Towne founded
1685—Madagascar rice introduced
1706—Forces of Spain and France turned back
1711—Beaufort founded
1715—Yamasee War
1718—Pirate threat controlled
1719—Carolina divided into North and South
1721—First royal governor appointed
1732—First South Carolina newspaper published
1736—Dock Street Theater built, first in country
1741—Middleton Place Gardens begun
1760—Cherokee War begins
1762—St. Cecilia Society founded
1765—South Carolina sends delegates to Stamp Act Congress
1773—Charleston Museum founded, oldest in the nation
1775—Royal governor flees; Provincial congress takes over
1776—William Moultrie saves Charleston from British
1780—British capture Charles Towne; Battle of Kings Mountain
1781—Battle of the Cowpens
1782—British withdraw from Charles Towne
1783—Charles Towne becomes Charleston
1789—First cotton mill in America built on James Island
1790—Capital moved to Columbia
1801—Beginning of the University of South Carolina
1830—First railroad built to use a steam engine
1832—Nullification ordinance passed
1846—Palmetto Regiment serves in Mexican War
1850—John C. Calhoun dies
1854—Statehouse is begun
1856—First State Fair
1860—Ordinance of Secession approved
1861—Confederate States of America formed; war begins with attack on Fort
    Sumter
1865—Columbia burned; war ends
1868—South Carolina readmitted to Union
1876—Wade Hampton election ends Reconstruction period
1886—Charleston suffers heavy earthquake
1895—State Constitution adopted
1907—Statehouse is finished
1917—World War I begins; 62,000 serve; 2,085 die

89

1918 — Remarkable adult education program begun
1921 — Boll weevil destroys much of cotton crop
1923 — Pioneer Parker School District created
1931 — Dreher Shoals Dam completed
1941 — World War II begins; Ervin David Shaw, of Sumter, one of the first
     American pilots killed; 173,642 serve
1945 — State Development Board created
1953 — Savannah nuclear plant begins production
1961 — Technical training centers program initiated
1965 — Industrial development exceeds $600,000,000 in year
1966 — Record tonnage handled in South Carolina ports
1975 — Governor James B. Edwards takes office, first Republican since
     Reconstruction
1979 — Democrats regain the state house

Thinkers, Doers, Fighters

People of renown who have been associated with South Carolina

Anderson, Richard H.
Bethune, Mary McLeod
Blue, Victor
Burr, Theodosia
Butler, Pierce
Calhoun, John Caldwell
Carlisle, James H.
Clemson, Thomas G.
Coker, David
Cooper, Thomas
Garden, Alexander
Hampton, Wade, III
Jackson, Andrew
Laurens, Henry
Marion, Francis
Mills, Robert
Moultrie, William
Parker, Francis L.

Peterkin, Julia
Pickens, Andrew
Pinckney, Charles
Pinckney, Charles Cotesworth
Pinckney, Thomas
Poinsett, Joel Robert
Purvis, Melvin
Roberts, Henry Martin
Rutledge, John
Springs, Elliott White
Strickland, Lily
Sumter, Thomas
Timrod, Henry
Waddel, Moses
Williams, David Rogerson
Wilson, John Leighton
Wofford, Benjamin
Woodward, Henry

90

Governors of the State of South Carolina (since statehood)

Thomas Pinckney 1787-1789
Charles Pinckney 1789-1792
William Moultrie 1792-1794
Arnoldus Vander Horst 1794-1796
Charles Pinckney 1796-1798
Edward Rutledge 1798-1800
John Drayton 1800-1802
James Burchill Richardson 1802-1804
Paul Hamilton 1804-1806
Charles Pinckney 1806-1808
John Drayton 1808-1810
Henry Middleton 1810-1812
Joseph Alston 1812-1814
David R. Williams 1814-1816
Andrew Pickens 1816-1818
John Geddes 1818-1820
Thomas Bennett 1820-1822
John Lyde Wilson 1822-1824
Richard Irvine Manning 1824-1826
John Taylor 1826-1828
Stephen D. Miller 1828-1830
James Hamilton, Jr. 1830-1832
Robert Y. Hayne 1832-1834
George McDuffie 1834-1836
Pierce Mason Butler 1836-1838
Patrick Noble 1838-1840
B.K. Henagan 1840
John Peter Richardson 1840-1842
James H. Hammond 1842-1844
William Aiken 1844-1846
David Johnson 1846-1848
Whitmarsh B. Seabrook 1848-1850
John Hugh Means 1850-1852
John Laurence Manning 1852-1854
James Hopkins Adams 1854-1856
Robert F.W. Allston 1856-1858
William H. Gist 1858-1860
Francis Wilkinson Pickens 1860-1862
Milledge Luke Bonham 1862-1864
Andrew Gordon Magrath 1864-1865
Benjamin Franklin Perry 1865

James Lawrence Orr 1865-1868
Robert K. Scott 1868-1872
Franklin J. Moses, Jr. 1872-1874
Daniel H. Chamberlain 1874-1876
Wade Hampton 1876-1879
William Dunlap Simpson 1879-1880
Thomas B. Jeter 1880
Johnson Hagood 1880-1882
Hugh Smith Thompson 1882-1886
John C. Sheppard 1886
John Peter Richardson 1886-1890
Benjamin Ryan Tillman 1890-1894
John Gary Evans 1894-1897
William H. Ellerbe 1897-1899
Miles B. McSweeney 1899-1903
Duncan Clinch Heyward 1903-1907
Martin F. Ansel 1907-1911
Coleman Livingston Blease 1911-1915
Charles A. Smith 1915
Richard Irvine Manning 1915-1919
Robert A. Cooper 1919-1922
Wilson G. Harvey 1922-1923
Thomas G. McLeod 1923-1927
John G. Richards, 1927-1931
Ibra C. Blackwood 1931-1935
Olin D. Johnston 1935-1939
Burnet R. Maybank 1939-1941
J.E. Harley 1941-1942
R.M. Jeffries 1942-1943
Olin D. Johnston 1943-1945
Ransome J. Williams 1945-1947
J. Strom Thurmond 1947-1951
James F. Byrnes 1951-1955
George Bell Timmerman, Jr. 1955-1959
Ernest F. Hollings 1959-1963
Donald S. Russell 1963-1967
Robert E. McNair 1967-1971
John C. West 1971-1975
James Burrows Edwards 1975-1979
Richard Riley 1979-

Index

**page numbers in bold type
indicate illustrations**

Abbeville County, 56
Abolitionists, 30, 31
Academy of Fine Arts,
    Charleston, 58
Adams, John Quincy, 56
Adult education, 69
Agriculture, 38, 39, 48-50
Aiken, 47, 83
Ainsly Hall Mansion,
    Columbia, 82
Albemarle Point, 19
Alston, Joseph, 61
Anderson, Richard H.
    (Fighting Dick), 61
Anderson, Robert, 86
Anderson (city), 35, 64, 65, 86
Anderson County, 86
Anderson County
    Courthouse, 86
Andrew Jackson Historical
    State Park, 85-86
Animals, 43
Anne, Queen of England, 20
Apalachee Indians, 16
Appalachia, 11
Archaic-Early Woodland
    people, 15
Architect, Federal, 64
Area of state, 11, 88
"Area Rehabilitation," 74
Artists, 64
Asbury, Francis, 40
Ashepoo Indians, 15
Ashley River, 12, 76
Atomic Energy Commission,
    83
Atomic energy plants, 47, **48**,
    83
Attakullakulla (Chief), 24
Audubon, John James, 41
Authors, 63, 64
Ayllón, Lucas Vásquez de, 17
Baedeker Guide, 77
Baruch, Bernard, 84
Bates, Clayton "Peg Leg," 87
Battle of Cowpens (painting),
    29
Beaufort, 33, 59, 79, 80
Beaufort County, 79
Beaufort Museum, 79
Beaufort water festival, **80**
Beauregard, P.G.T., 32
Belle Island Gardens,
    Georgetown, 81
Belle Isle, 9

Benedict College, 68, 82
Bennettsville, 49
Benton, Thomas Hart, 56
Berkeley County, 9, 58
Best Friend of Charleston, The
    (locomotive), 51
Bethune, Mary McLeod, 69
Big Apple (dance), 72
Bird, state, **87**, 88
Birds, **41**, 44, 79
Bishopville, 84
Blackbeard, 21, 72
Black River, 12
Blacks, 38, 40, 62, 64, 65
"Bloody Tarleton," 26, **27**
Blue, Victor, 61
Bluefields Plantation, 61
Blue granite, 46, 50
Blue Ridge Mountains, 11
Blue Ridge Province, 11
Blue Savanna, Battle of, 84
Bohicket Indians, 15
Boll weevil, 39
Bolt, Oliver, 86
Bonnet, Stede, 21, 22, 74
Bonney, Ann, 74
Boozer, Marie, 65
Bristol (ship), 25
Broad River, 12
Broad Road, Columbia, 34
Brookgreen Gardens,
    Georgetown, 81
Brooks, Preston S., 83
Bryant, William Cullen, 10
Buffalo (town), 43
Buffington, Willie Lee, 65
Buford, Abraham, 26
Bull, John, 80
Bull Bay, 15
Bull Island, 12, 45, 79
Burr, Aaron, 61
Burr, Theodosia, 61, 62
Butler, Pierce, 29
Buxton Brothers, 82
Byrnes, James J., 57
Calhoun, John C., 30, **54**, 56,
    57, 67, 74
California, 56, 57
Camden, 9, 84
Camden, Battle of, 55, 84
Campbell, William, 25, 28
Camp Wadsworth, 38
Canals, 52
Cape Romain National
    Refuge, 44, 79
Capitals, state, 29, 81
Capitol building, state, 82, **83**

Carlisle, James H., 69
Carolina Bays, 81
Carolina *Gazette,* 52, 53
Carolina Homespun Co., 47
Carolina otters, 43
Carolina Power and Light, 47
Carpetbaggers, 36, **36**
Castle Pinckney, 32
Casualties, war, 30, 34, 38
Catawba Indian Reservation,
    40, 86
Catawba Indians, 15, 40, 84,
    86
Catawba Lake, 12
Catawba River, 12
Cayce, 82
Chamberlain, Daniel H., 37
Charles I, King of England, 18
Charles II, King of England, 18
Charleston, 9, 18, 19, 20, 21,
    21, 22, 23, 24, 25, 26, 29,
    30, 31, 32, 33, 34, 38, 39,
    40, 44, 45, 47, 51, 52, **53**,
    58, 59, 60, 63, 64, 67, 69,
    70, 71-77, **73**, **75**, 81
Charleston (dance), 72
Charleston *Courier,* 51
Charleston Museum, 72
Charles Towne (Charleston),
    19, 20, 21, **21**, 22, 23, 24,
    25, 26, 29, 63
Chattooga River, 12
Cheraw, 84
Cheraw Indians, 15
Cherokee County, 51
Cherokee Indians, 15, 16, 17,
    18, 22, 23, 24, 25, 29, 60
Chicken, George, 20
Children's Nature Museum,
    Rock Hill, 85
Christmas Carellon,
    Columbia, 82
Chronology, 89, 90
Churches, 31, 74, 80, 81, 84
Church of England, 40
Citadel, The (college), 32, 67,
    68
Cities, principal, 88
City Hall, Camden, 84
City Hall, Charleston, 74
"City of Famous Gateways,"
    75
Civil War, 31-34, 61
Claflin College, 68
Clarendon County, 81
Clark, Mark, 67
Clark Hill Reservoir, 12

Clay, Henry, 57
Clays, 46, 50
Clemson, Thomas G., 67
Clemson (city), 67
Clemson University, 67
Cleveland, Benjamin, 28
Clifton, 65
Climate, 13
Clinton, Henry, 25
Clinton (town), 65, 68
Clover (town), 85
Coastal Plain, 11, 46
Coastline, state, 12, 88
Cofitachiqui, Princess, 17
Coker, David, 50, 62
College of Charleston, 67
Colleges, 67, 68
Columbia, 30, 31, 33, 34, 37,
    50, 52, 64, 65, 67, 68, 81, 82
Columbia College, 68, 82
Columbia Museum of Art and
    Science, 82
Columbia *The State,* 52
Combahee Indians, 15
Combahee River, 12
Commission-City Manager
    Plan, 38
Commons House of
    Representatives, 24
Communication, 52, 53
Composers, 64
Confederate Museum,
    Charleston, 76
Confederate States of
    America, 31
Congaree Indians, 15
Congaree River, 12
Congress, U.S., 30, 56, 58, 64,
    65
Conrad, Arthur, 54
Constitutional Convention,
    29, 60
Constitution, U.S., 29, 35, 59,
    60
Constitutions, state, 35, 38
Coogler, J. Gordon, 63
Cooglerism, 63
Cooper, Anthony Ashley, 76
Cooper, Thomas, 30
Cooper River, 12, 76
Coosa Indians, 15
Coosawatchie River, 12
Corn, 49
Cornwallis, Lord Charles, 9,
    25, 28, 61
Corruption of the Carpetbaggers
    (cartoon), **36**

Cotton, 38, 47, 48, 49, 62
Cowpens, Battle of the, 28, **29**, 37, 85
Cowpens National Battlefield Military Park, 85
Craven, Charles, 20
Crops, 48-50
Cuming, Alexander, 22, 23
Cunningham, Ann Pamela, 65
Cusabo Confederacy, 15
Cypress Gardens, Charleston, **42**, 77, 79
Dams, 12, 39, 86
Darby Plantation, **14**
Dean Hall Plantation, 79
Declaration of Independence, 25
Delegation of Cherokee Chiefs, 1730 (painting), **18**
Density of population, 88
Deserters, war, 34
De Soto, Hernando, 17
Dingles Mill, 34
Disasters, 23, 38, 72
Disease, 23, 31
Dock Street Theater, Charleston, 72
Drake, Frederick, 49
Drayton family, 79
Dreher Shoals, 52
Dreher Shoals Dam, 39
Dueling, 84
Due West, 68
Duke Power Co., 47
Earthquakes, 38
Edgefield, 38, 83
Edisto Gardens, Orangeburg, 83
Edisto Indians, 15
Edisto Island, 12, 31, 79
Edisto River, 12
Edmunsbon-Alston House, 74
Education, 67-69
Edwards, James B., 39
Ellenton, 36
England, 17, 18, 19, 20, 23, 24, 60
Episcopal church, 19
Erskine College, 68
Esaw Indians, 15
Ethnic groups, 40
Etiwan Indians, 15
Evans, Mathilda, 62
Exchange Building, Charleston, 75, **75**
Fall Line, 11, 22
Farmers Society Building, Anderson, 86
Farming, 38, 39, 48-50
Farragut, David G., 76
Federal Arsenal, Charleston, 32
Ferguson, Patrick, 28

First Baptist Church, Columbia, 31
First Continental Congress, 24
Fish, 43, 44
Fish, state, 88
Flag, state, 25, 44
Florence County, 81
Flower, state, 45, **87**, 88
Flowers, 45, 58, 59, 77, 79
Folly Island, 33
Forests, 44, 45, 47
Fort Johnson, 24
Fort Mill, 47
Fort Motte, 63, 83, 84
Fort Moultrie, 25, 32, 77
Fort Prince George, 23, 24
Fort Sumter, 32, **33, 76**
Fort Sumter National Monument, 76
Fort Watson, 27
Fort White, 81
Fossils, 11, 46
Foster, Stephen, 81
Foster's Tavern, Spartanburg, 85
Fountain Inn, 87
4-H clubs, 83
Fourteenth Amendment, U.S. Constitution, 35
France, 17, 18, 20, 38, 61
Francis Marion National Forest, 45
Francis Marion Offers His Humble Meal (painting), **8**
Franklin, Benjamin, 53
French and Indian War, 23
Fripp Island, 12, 43
Fundamental Constitutions, 19
Gabriel's Plantation, 9
Gaffney, 28, 85
Gaillard, Peter, 48
Galsworthy, John, 77
"Gamecock, The," 27, 61
Garden, Alexander, 59
Gardenias, 59
Gardens, 71, 74, 77, 79, 81, 83, 84
Gates, Horatio, 26
Geographic center, state, 88
Geography, 11
Geology, 11
George II, King of England, 81
Georgetown, 40, 52, 61, 81
Georgetown Neck, 43
Georgia, 12
Gershwin, George, 64
Gibbes, James S., 72
Gibbes Art Gallery, Charleston, 72
Gillespie, Jesse B., 38
Gist, States Rights, 31
Gist, William H., 31

Goatfield Plantation, 9
Gold, 45, 46, 51
Goodwyn, Mayor, 34
Gorilla, discoverer of, 62
Governors, state, 31, 32, 35, 37, 38, 39, 57, 59, 60, 61, 62, 83, 91
Grand Strand, 81
Gray, Wil Lou, 69
Gray-Man ghost, 79
"Great Mortality" of 1749, 23
"Great Warrior, The," 23
Greene, Nathanael, 9, 28
Greenville, 31, 34, 35, 69, 85
Greenwood Lake, 12
Grimké, Sarah and Angelina, 31
Growing season, 13
Guerrillas, 9, 26, 27, 57, 60
Gullah dialect, 40
Hagood, Johnson, 61
Haigler (Chief), 84
Haile gold mine, 51
Hampton, Wade, 30, 34, 82
Hampton, Wade III, 36, 37, 60, 65, 82
Hampton-Preston House, 82
Hartford (Farragut's flagship), 76
Hartsville nuclear center, **48**
Hartwell Dam, 86
Hartwell Reservoir, 12, 86
Hayes, Rutherford B., 37
Haynesworth, George E., 32
Haywood-Washington House, 74
Heath, Robert, 18
Heyward, DuBose, 64, 71
Heyward, Thomas, Jr., 25
Highest point, state, 11, 88
High Shoals, 86
Highways, 52
Hill, Daniel H., 61
Hilton Head Island, 12, 43, 44, 79
Historic Charleston Foundation, 74
Hogologee Indians, 16
Holly Hill, 47
Honey Chile, 64
Horry, P., 10
Huguenots, 17, 74
Hunting Island, 12
Hurricane Shoals, 65
Hydrogen bomb, 83
Immigration, 22
Independent Republic of Texas, 56
Indian Hill, 15
Indians, 11, 15-17, 18, **18**, 19, 20, 22, 23, 24, 25, 28, 29, 40, 45, 60, 63, 77, 84, 86
Indigo, 19, 48

Industry, 47, 48
Interstate and West Indian Exposition, 38
Intracoastal Waterway, 52
Inventors, 62
Iroquois Indians, 16
Islands, 12, 79
Isle of Palms, 12
Jackson, Andrew, 30, 55, 56, 64, 85
Jackson, Andrew, Sr., 55
Jacobs, William Plumer, 65
Jaggers, Charles, 64
Jaggers Old Folks' Home for Negroes, 64
James Island, 47
Jamison, D.F., 31
Jasper, William, 25
Jefferson, 46
Jenkins, Daniel J., 64
Jenkins Institute, 64
Jewish population, 40, 74
John P. Grace Memorial Bridge, Charleston, 77
Johnson, Andrew, 36, 86
Johnson, Henrietta, 64
Johnson, Nathaniel, 20
Johnson, Robert, 21, 22
Jolly, Manse, 65
Jones, Solomon, 62
Judaism, Reformed, 40
Kahal Kadosh Beth Elohim synagogue, Charleston, 74
Kalb, Baron de, 84
Keowee, 23
Kershaw, 46, 51
Kiawah Indians, 15
Kings Creek, 46
Kings Mountain, Battle of, 28, 85
Kings Mountain National Military Park, 85, **86**
Lake Marion, 12
Lake Moultrie, 12
Lakes, 12, **13**
Lancaster, 26, 55, 63
Lands Ford, 52
Lanford Station, 50
Laurens, Henry, 61
Laurens, John, 61
Laurens (town), 36, 86
Laurens County, 50
Layton, Mary, 74
Lee, Stephen D., 61
Legislatures, state, 35, 37, 47, 56, 62
Lehman, George, 41
Length, greatest, state, 88
Lincoln, Benjamin, 26
Lindy Lou, 64
Little Pee Dee River, 12
Locke, John, 19
Lockheed Aviation Co., 47

London, England, 17
Long Cane Massacre, 24
Long Cane region, 56
Longstreet, James, 61
Lords proprietors, 19, 20, 22, 48
Low-country region, 11, 39
Lowest point, state, 88
Lumbering, 47
Lunches River, 12
Lynch, Thomas, Jr., 25
Madagascar rice, 19, 48, 63
Magnolia Gardens, Charleston, 59, 77
Magrath, A.G., 35
Manigault, Joseph, 74
Manning, Elizabeth Peyre Richardson, 60
Manning, Richard I., 60
Manufacturing, 47, 48
Marines, U.S., 81
Marion, Francis, 8, 9, 10, 26, 27, 45, 57, 58, 81, 84
Marion (town), 61, 84
Market Hall, Charleston, 76
Mayesville, 69
McCormick, 46
McKissic Library, University of South Carolina, 66
Medical University of South Carolina, 67
Memoirs of the Revolution, 60
Mepkin Estate, 61
Methodism, 40
Mexican War, 30, 82
Mexico, 58
Michaux, 77
Middleton, Arthur, 25, 77
Middleton, Henry, 77
Middleton Place Gardens, Charleston, 77, 78
Midlands region, 11
Mills, Clark, 64
Mills, Robert, 64, 82
Minerals and mining, 45, 46, 50, 51
Moore, James, 22
Morgan, Daniel, 28, 85
Morris Island, 32, 33
Motte, Rebecca, 83
Mottoes, state, 88
Moultrie, Hugh, 60
Moultrie, William, 25, 60, 76
Mound builders, 15
Mountains, 11
Mount Vernon Ladies Assn., 65
Mullins, 84
Murray Lake, 12
Museums, 71, 72, 76, 79, 82, 85
Myrtle Beach, 45, 81
National forests, 45

National Institution for the Promotion of Science, 58
National monument, 76
National Society of Colonial Dames, 76
National refuge, 44, 79
Newberry, 68
Newberry College, 68
New Orleans, Battle of, 30, 87
Newspapers, 52
Nickname, state, 45, 88
North Carolina, 12, 55
Nuclear power plants, 47, 48, 83
Nullification, 30, 55
Nunda Wadigi Indians, 16
Oaks, The (plantation), 61
Oconee County, 50, 86
"Old Reformer, The" (cannon), 86
Old Slave Mart Museum and Gallery, Charleston, 76
Orangeburg, 67, 68, 83
Ordinance of Nullification, 55
Ordinance of Secession, 31, 86
Orphanages, 65
Orr, James L., 35
Oseola (Chief), 77
Pakenham, General, 87
Palmetto Regiment, 30, 82
Palmettos, 44
"Palmetto State," 44
Paris Mountain State Park, 85
Parker, Peter, 25
Parker, Francis L., 62
Parker District School, 69
Parks, 71, 81, 85, 86
Parr, 47
Parris Island, 17, 81
Patapsco (Union ship), 32, 77
Patriot (schooner), 61, 62
Pawleys Island, 79
Peaches, 50
Peedee Indians, 15
Pee Dee River, 9, 12, 81
People, 39, 40, 90
Perry, Benjamin F., 31, 35
Peterkin, Julia, 63
Peyre Plantation, 9
Pickens, Andrea Dorothea, 66
Pickens, Andrew, 27, 29, 60
Pickens, Francis, 32
Pickens (town), 23, 38
Pickens County Courthouse, 38
Piedmont region, 11, 28, 85
Pinckney, Charles, 29, 59
Pinckney, Charles (Constitutional Convention delegate), 60
Pinckney, Charles Cotesworth, 29, 59
Pinckney, Thomas, 59

Pineville, 81
Pirates, 20, 21, 22, 62, 72, 74
Planter (ship), 65
Planters Hotel, Charleston, 72
Planters Punch (drink), 72
Plants, 44, 45, 58, 59, 77
Pocotaligo, 20
Poinsett, Joel Robert, 58, 59
Poinsettias, 59
Polo Capital of the South, 83
Pond Bluff Plantation, 9
Population figures, 40, 88
Porgy, 64
Porgy and Bess, 64
Port Royal, 20, 33, 52
Port Royal Sound, 52
Ports, 39, 52, 53
Pratt, John, 62
Prehistoric times, 11, 15
Presbyterian College, 65, 68
Presidents, U.S., 30, 36, 37, 38, 55, 56, 86
Prince George Winyah Church, Georgetown, 81
Provost Dungeon, Charleston, 75
Pulitzer Prize, 63
Purvis, Melvin, 65
Raccoons, 43
Race riots, 36
Railroads, 33, 51, 85
Rainbow Division, World War I, 38
Rainbow Row, Charleston, 74
Rainfall, 13
Ravenel, Henry William, 62
Reconstruction, 35, 36, 37, 65
Red House, Walhalla, 60
Red Shirts, 37, 65
Reformed Judaism, 40
Reformed Society of Israelites, 40
Religion, 40
Reservoirs, 12
Revolutionary War, 9, 10, 25-29, 55, 60, 65
Reynolds, Joshua, 27
Rhett, William, 21
Ribaut, Jean, 17, 52
Rice, 19, 48, 63
Richardson-Manning family, 60
Rivers, 12, 52
Roads, 52, 62
Roberts, Bishop, 21
Roberts, Henry Martin, 63
Roberts Rules of Order, 63
Robertsville, 63
Robin Hood of the Revolution, 9
Rock Hill, 40, 67, 85, 86
Rock Mount, 52
Rocks Plantation, The, 48

Rocky River, 86
Roosevelt, Theodore, 38
Royal colony, 22
"Rule of the Robbers," 35
Russell, Nathaniel, House, 74
Rutledge, Edward, 25
Rutledge, John, 29
Sachems, 15, 16
Sahkanga (mountains), 11
St. Cecilia Society, 72
St. David's Church, Cheraw, 84
St. George's Bay, 18
St. Helena Indians, 15
St. Helena Island, 40
St. Helena's Church, Beaufort, 80
St. John's Church, Charleston, 74
St. John's Parish, 9
St. Mary's Church, Charleston, 74
St. Michael's Church, Charleston, 32, 74
St. Philip's Church, Charleston, 74
St. Stephens, 20
Saluda River, 12, 39
Sampit Indians, 15
Sand Hills, 46
San Miguel de Gualdape, 17
Santee Canal, 52
Santee-Cooper Dam, 12
Santee-Cooper Lake, 12
Santee Indians, 15
Santee River, 9, 12, 58, 60
Sassafras Mountain, 11
Savannah River, 12, 15
Savannah River Plant, Atomic Energy Commission, 83
Sayle, William, 19
Scalawags, 36
Scarlet Sister Mary, 63
Schools, 69
Scientists, 62, 63
Scotch-Irish, 28
Scotts Lake Indian Mound, 84
Secession, 30, 31
Secession Ordinance, 86
Second Contienental Congress, 24
Secretaries of State, 56, 57, 59
Secretaries of War, 56, 58, 59
Seewee Indians, 15, 16
Seewee Indian Shell Mound, 15
Senators, U.S., 38, 56, 57
Sevier, John, 28
Shaw, Ervin David, 39
Shaw Air Force Base, 39, 84
Shecut, Carolina Homespun, 47
Shecut, L.E.W., 47

Shelby, Isaac, 28
Sherman, William T., 33, 34, 82
Shoreline, state, 12, 88
Siegler, Marie, 83
Silver Bluff, 17
Simms, William Gilmore, 63
Simpkins, Eury, 65
Sims, J. Marion, 62
Sioux Indians, 15
Skyagusta (Wizard Owl), 60
Slavery, 19, 30, 31, 34, 35, 56
Smalls, Robert, 65
Smith, Alice R.H., 64
Smith, Reed, 40
Smithsonian Institution, 58
Smyrna, 46
Snow Island, 9
Song, state, 88
Songs, 40, 64
South Carolina, A Guide to the Palmetto State, 35
South Carolina College, 67
South Carolina State College, 67
Southern Textile Exposition, 85
Spain, 17, 18, 20, 59
Spanish American War, 61
Spartanburg, 37, 38, 50, 67, 85
Spartan Regiment, 85
Springs, Elliott White, 63
Springs Cotton Mills, 47, 63
Stamp Act Congress, 24
Star of the West (ship), 32
Stateburg, 84
State Development Board, 39
State Fair, 82
State Farmers Markets, 50
Statehood, 29
Statehouse, 82, **83**

State parks, 71, 81, 85, 86
Statistics, 88
Stone, state, 88
Stono Indians, 15
Stono River, 20
Strickland, Lily, 64
Submarine warfare, 32
Sullivans Island, 12, 25
Summerville, 50
Sumner, Charles, 83
Sumter, Thomas, 27, 60, 84
Sumter (town), 32, 37, 38, 39, 84
Sumter County, 81
Sumter National Forest, 45
Suwanee River, FL, 81
"Swamp Fox," 10, 26, 27, 81
Swan Lake Iris Gardens, Sumter, 84
Sword Gate House, Charleston, 75
Symbol, state, 88
Table Rock, 86
Tarleton, Banastre, 26, 27, **27**, 28
"Tea party," Charles Towne, 24
Technical training, 69
Temperatures, 13
Texas, 56
Textiles, 47, 85
Thirteenth Amendment, U.S. Constitution, 35
Thomas, Jane, 65
Thomas, Paul and T.M., 85
Thornwell Orphanage, 65
Tillman, Benjamin R. (Pitchfork), 38
Timmonsville, 65
Timothee, Lewis, 53

Timothy, Elizabeth, 53
Timrod, Henry, 63
Tin, 51
Tobacco, 49, **49**, 84
Topographic regions, 11
Tories, 25, 28
Transportation, 51, 52
Treasury Building, Washington, D.C., 64
Tree, state, 88
Trees, 44, 45
Trescot, William Henry, 34
Trinity Episcopal Church, Columbia, 81
Tugaloo River, 12
Tyler, John, 56
Typewriter, invention of, 62
Unitarian church, Charleston, 74
United States Navy Yard, Charleston, 77
Universities, 67
University of South Carolina, **66**, 67, 82
Up-country region, 11, 39, 52, 81, 85
Van Buren, Martin, 56
Vermiculite, 46, 50
Verner, Elizabeth O'Neill, 64
Vice President, U.S., 56
Waccamaw River, 12
Wadboo plantation, 58
Waddell, Moses, 69
Walhalla, 60
Wando Indians, 15
War of 1812, 30, 62
Washington, George, 61, 65, 75
Washington Monument, Washington, D.C., 64

Wateree Indians, 15
Wateree Lake 12
Wateree River, 12
Waxhaw Indians, 15
Waxhaw Presbyterian cemetery, 55
Weems, Parson Mason Locke, 10, 58
West, Joseph, 19
West Columbia, 82
Westo Indians, 15
West Springs, 46
White, John Blake, 8, 10
Whitepoint Gardens, Charleston, 74
Whitewater Falls, 86
Whitner, W.C., 86
Width, greatest, state, 88
Williams, David Rogerson, 50, 62
Wilson, John Leighton, 62
Wilson, Woodrow, 82
Wilson's Snipe (painting), **41**
Wimbee Indians, 15
Winnsboro, 46, 50, 84
Winthrop College, 67
Winyah Bay, 17
Winyah Indians, 15
Wofford, Benjamin, 67
Wofford College, 67, 69
Woods Bay State Park, 81
Woodward, Henry, 19, 63
Woodward (town), 87
World War I, 38, 63
World War II, 39
Worley, Richard, 21, 22, 74
Yamasee Indians, 15, 16, 22
Yamasee War, 20
York, 28
York County, 85
Yuchi Indians, 16

PICTURE CREDITS

ABOUT THE AUTHOR

With the publication of his first book for school use when he was twenty, **Allan Carpenter** began a career as an author that has spanned more than 135 books. After teaching in the public schools of Des Moines, Mr. Carpenter began his career as an educational publisher at the age of twenty-one when he founded the magazine *Teachers Digest*. In the field of educational periodicals, he was responsible for many innovations. During his many years in publishing, he has perfected a highly organized approach to handling large volumes of factual material: after extensive traveling and having collected all possible materials, he systematically reviews and organizes everything. From his apartment high in Chicago's John Hancock Building, Allan recalls, "My collection and assimilation of materials on the states and countries began before the publication of my first book." Allan is the founder of Carpenter Publishing House and of Infordata International, Inc., publishers of *Issues in Education* and *Index to U. S. Government Periodicals*. When he is not writing or traveling, his principal avocation is music. He has been the principal bassist of many symphonies, and he managed the country's leading non-professional symphony for twenty-five years.